PENGUIN BOOKS
1188
AGAINST THE LAW
PETER WILDEBLOOD

AGAINST THE LAW

PETER WILDEBLOOD

PENGUIN BOOKS

Penguin Books Ltd, Harmondsworth, Middlesex
AUSTRALIA: Penguin Books Pty Ltd, 762 Whitehorse Road,
Mitcham, Victoria

—

First published by Weidenfeld and Nicholson 1955
Published in Penguin Books 1957
Reprinted 1957, 1959

Made and printed in Great Britain
by Hunt, Barnard & Co. Ltd,
Aylesbury

FOR MY MOTHER AND FATHER

Although one of the charges made against me was one of conspiracy, there was, and has been, no conspiracy. The views expressed in this book are entirely and exclusively my own ; there has been no consultation with anybody else.

P. W.

PART ONE

SOMETIMES, when a man is dying, he directs that his body shall be given to the doctors, so that the causes of his suffering and death may be investigated, and the knowledge used to help others. I cannot give my body yet; only my heart and my mind, trusting that by this gift I can give some hope and courage to other men like myself, and to the rest of the world some understanding.

I am a homosexual. It is easy for me to make that admission now, because much of my private life has already been made public by the newspapers. I am in the rare, and perhaps privileged, position of having nothing left to hide. My only concern is that some good may come at last out of so much evil, and with that end in view I shall set down what happened to me as faithfully and fairly as I can. I do not pity myself, and I do not ask for pity. If there is bitterness in this book, I hope it will be the bitterness of medicine, not of poison.

The case in which I was involved has become known as the 'Montagu Case'; because one of the accused men was a peer, it received a great deal of publicity. But in essentials, it was not very different from hundreds of cases which come before the courts every year. These attract little attention, but each of them implies the downfall, and perhaps the ruin, of a human being. In the last few years there has been much discussion of this question, and many authoritative men and women have given their views about the prevalence, nature, prevention, punishment, and cure of homosexuality. There have not, I think, been any among them who could say, as I do now: 'I am a homosexual.' For what it is worth, I should like to offer, with all humility, this account of my life, my trial, my imprisonment and return to freedom as a contribution to the study of an urgent and tragic problem which affects many thousands of men.

I am no more proud of my condition than I would be of having a glass eye or a hare-lip. On the other hand, I am no more ashamed of it than I would be of being colour-blind or of writing with my left hand. It is essentially a personal problem, which only becomes a matter of public concern when the law makes it so. For many years I kept it a secret from my family and friends, not so much from choice as from expediency, and I tried privately to resolve my own struggle in a way as consistent as possible with the moral law. During that time I do not believe I ever did any harm to anyone else; if any harm has been done since, I do not think the fault lies with me, but rather with those who dragged out into the merciless light of publicity things which would have been better left in darkness. When the searchlights of the law were turned on to my life, only a part of it was illuminated. I am not proud of what was exposed; most people, if they were honest, would admit that their private lives would not bear such a relentless scrutiny. It will be my task, therefore, to turn on more lights, revealing, in place of the blurred and shadowy figure of the newspaper photographs, a man differing from other men only in one respect.

I must begin by trying to show what this difference is. The whole question is so surrounded by ignorance, moral horror and misunderstanding that it is not easy to approach it with an open mind. I shall not try, at this stage, either to explain or to excuse it, but simply to describe my condition. Briefly, it is that I am attracted towards men, in the way in which most men are attracted towards women. I am aware that many people, luckier than myself, will read this statement with incredulity and perhaps with derision; but it is the simple truth. This peculiarity makes me a social misfit from the start; I know that it cannot ever be entirely accepted by the rest of the community, and I do not ask that it should. It is up to me to come to terms, first with my own condition, and secondly with other people whose lives quite rightly centre upon the relationship between a man and a woman. If it was possible for me to become like them I should do so; and nothing would be easier for me than to assume a superficial normality, get married and perhaps have a family. This would, however, be at best dishonest, because I should be running away from my own problem, and at worst it would be cruel, because I should run the risk of making two people unhappy instead of one.

I think it is more honest, and less harmful, for a man with homosexual tendencies to recognize himself for what he is. He will always be lonely; he must accept that. He will never know the companionship that comes with marriage, or the joy of watching his children grow up, but he will at least have the austere consolations of self-knowledge and integrity. More than that he cannot have, because the law, in England, forbids it. A man who feels an attraction towards other men is a social misfit only; once he gives way to that attraction, he becomes a criminal.

This is not the case in most other countries, where the behaviour of consenting adults in private is considered a matter for themselves alone. Britain and America are almost the only countries in which such behaviour constitutes an offence, and in America the law is reduced to absurdity by the fact that it applies officially, also, to a variety of acts between men and women, whether married or not; it has been estimated that a strict application of the law would result in the imprisonment of two-thirds of the adult population, and as a result it is seldom invoked, even against homosexuals.

In Britain, however, the law is very much alive, and heavy penalties are incurred by anyone who breaks it. A homosexual who gives way to his impulses, even if he is doing no conceivable harm to anyone, therefore runs appalling risks. The fact that so many men do so shows that the law, however savage, is no deterrent. If, as people sometimes say, homosexuality is nothing but an affectation assumed by idle men who wish to be considered 'different', it is indeed strange that men should run the risk of life imprisonment in order to practise it.

The truth is that an adult man who has chosen a homosexual way of life has done so because he knows that no other course is open to him. It is easy to preach chastity when you are not obliged to practise it yourself, and it must be remembered that, to a homosexual, there is nothing intrinsically shameful or sinful in his condition. Everywhere he goes, he sees other men like himself, forbidden by the law to give any physical expres-

9

sion to their desires. It is not surprising that he should seek a partner among them, so that together they may build a shelter against the hostile world. One of the charges often levelled against homosexuals is that they tend to form a compact and exclusive group. They can hardly be expected to do anything else, since they are legally excluded from the rest of the community.

In spite of this, it is difficult to draw a distinct line between homosexuals and 'normal' or heterosexual men. Many men have had homosexual experiences of one kind or another in the course of their lives without becoming exclusively homosexual. Probably large numbers of people go through a stage of this kind during childhood or adolescence, but sooner or later they make the natural transition into normality. This may be part of the process of growing up. A baby is interested in nothing but itself; a small child directs its affection towards other people regardless of their sex; an adolescent boy begins to feel attracted exclusively towards girls; a grown man chooses a woman as his partner. That is the normal pattern. In some cases, however, the process is arrested or reversed. The man remains as the child was, failing to discriminate between the sexes; or he develops in the abnormal direction of being attracted only towards his own sex.

Such desires can never, I believe, be wholly eradicated. They may perhaps be prevented from developing in the adolescent, if they are discovered soon enough, but it seems that little can be done for an adult who has these tendencies. I have consulted a great many psychiatrists and read dozens of books on the subject, without discovering much ground for hope. Doctors are, of course, always unwilling to admit defeat, but I have never yet found one who claimed to be able to turn a homosexual into a normal man. The most they can do, it seems, is to teach the ill-adjusted homosexual to accept his condition and make the best of a bad job; and this, of course, is directly contrary to the spirit of the law.

The view of the law – and it is shared by many sincere men and women – is that homosexuality is a monstrous perversion deliberately chosen, and that the men who make that choice deserve to be punished for it. The very words of the law are impregnated with emotion on this subject; murder is merely murder, but homosexual acts are 'the abominable crime' and 'gross indecency'. The upholders of the law will claim that homosexuality has always been a symptom of a nation's decadence, forgetting that it is widespread and tolerated in such respectable and progressive places as Switzerland and Scandinavia. They will say that it is inseparable from effeminacy, ignoring the fact that it has been practised among the most warlike communities, from the Samurai of medieval Japan to the present-day Pathans of the Northwest Frontier, and that men like Julius Caesar, Frederick the Great, and Lawrence of Arabia are known to have been homosexuals. They will argue that homosexuals are by nature vicious and depraved, because they cannot know that this minority group, branded by them as 'immoral', has an austere and strict morality of its own.

I suppose that most people, if they were asked to define the crime of Oscar Wilde, would still imagine that he was an effeminate poseur who lusted after small boys, whereas in fact he was a married man with two children who was found guilty of homosexual acts committed in private with male prostitutes whom he certainly did not corrupt. The Prosecution never attempted to prove that he had done any harm by his actions. It is arguable, however, that an immense amount of harm has been done during the last sixty years by the Wilde legend. In every generation there have probably been hundreds of adolescents who have been first puzzled, and then unwholesomely fascinated, by the aura of secrecy and sordid glamour which still surrounds the case. If Oscar Wilde had never been brought to trial, he would be remembered only as a minor poet and playwright; as it is, he has become a martyr.

This is doubly unfortunate because, as I have said, Wilde is falsely invested in most people's minds with the attributes of effeminacy and love of boys. The labels stick, even when we know that they do not tell the truth; and since Wilde is probably the best-known of all homosexuals, it is supposed that all of them share the tendencies which have, quite wrongly as it happens, been ascribed to him.

There are, of course, men whose sexual feelings are directed towards boys, just as there are 'normal' men who are attracted towards small girls. I have talked to many of them in prison, and I am more convinced than ever that they form a quite separate group from men like myself. Although I regard them with just as much distaste as anyone else, I have tried very hard to understand their point of view, but we have no common ground for discussion. My preferences are as inexplicable to them as theirs are to me. I do not pretend to know what is to be done with men like this; they must obviously be prevented from giving way to their inclinations, because of the harm that they may do, but I am not sure that imprisonment provides the answer.

It sems to me very important to discriminate between the pederast, or lover of boys, and the homosexual, or lover of men. I am not convinced that a boy can be turned into a permanent homosexual by an isolated, early experience, but this risk must at all costs be avoided. Furthermore, it seems fundamentally immoral to me for a man to take advantage of his greater age and experience to seduce a child, whether a boy or girl. Sexual experiences of any kind play such an important part in a person's development that they should not be allowed to take place until he or she is physically and mentally ready for them.

Homosexuality between adults presents a very different moral problem. There are thousands of men in this condition, who are forbidden by the law to seek any sexual outlet, even with one another. To the homosexual, this seems unjust. He does not wish to seduce children, not only because it seems to him basically immoral to do so, but because he is not attracted towards them. He is unlikely to make advances to 'normal' adults, because he knows that such men, even if he finds them attractive, will not want to have anything to do with him. Even if it were possible, he would not wish to take a 'normal' man away from his wife and family and persuade him to take up a way of life which he would always regret. On the other hand, he cannot see why he should be condemned to perpetual continence, when there are so many other men like himself with whom it would be possible to enter into a relationship which would do no harm to anyone.

That is the morality of the homosexual, and it is my own. It is not endorsed by the law of the country, as the best kind of relationship between a man and a woman is endorsed; in fact, as I shall show, the present state of the law actually goes far to discourage homosexual relationships of the more sincere and 'moral' kind. Nor is it much encouraged by the community: when all homosexual acts, whether between adult men or between men and boys, are treated by the law with equal severity, it is difficult for the general public to discriminate between them.

There is another misconception which I should like to dispel. This concerns the appearance and manner of the homosexual. Everyone has seen the pathetically flamboyant pansy with the flapping wrists, the common butt of music-hall jokes and public-house stories. Most of us are not like that. We do our best to look like everyone else, and we usually succeed. That is why nobody realizes how many of us there are. I know many hundreds of homosexuals and not more than half a dozen would be recognized by a stranger for what they are. If anything, they dress more soberly and behave more conventionally in public than the 'normal' men I know; they have to, if they are to avoid suspicion.

When I ask for tolerance, it is for men like these. Not the corrupters of youth, not even the effeminate creatures who love to make an exhibition of themselves, although by doing so they probably do no harm; I am only concerned with the men who, in spite of the tragic disability which is theirs, try to lead their lives according to the principles which I have described. They cannot speak for themselves, but I shall try to speak for them. Although I have been to prison and most of them have not, it is they who are the captives of circumstance, not I.

*

The Montagu Case, it will be remembered, was concerned with acts said to have been committed by five adults: Lord Montagu of Beaulieu, Michael Pitt-Rivers, Edward McNally, John Reynolds, and myself. The result of it was that three of us were sent to prison and the other two, as a reward for turning Queen's Evidence against us, were allowed to go free.

Much was made by the Prosecution of the difference in social status between the various people concerned in the case, and perhaps I should begin this account of my life with a description of my social background and of the childhood influences which made me what I became.

I was born at Alassio on the Italian Riviera in 1923. My father was a retired engineer from the Indian Public Works Department, who was at that time secretary of a tennis club patronized by the English visitors to the resort. My mother was the daughter of a sheep-rancher in the Argentine. She was many years younger than him, and I have often wondered whether this was one of the factors which influenced my later development; but I would never think of blaming them for what happened to me. They gave me all their love when I was a child, and their unquestioning loyalty at the time when I needed it most; I do not think that any parents could do more.

When I was three years old we came to live in London, and the family album shows a procession of cloche hats and silk-stockinged knees. There were going to be no more wars; the night-clubs were crowded and everyone danced the Charleston. The first songs I remember were 'Ramona', 'Charmaine', and 'A Room with a View', which was said to be a favourite of the Prince of Wales.

The various nannies who held dominion over my nursery were always talking about the Prince of Wales. I hated them all. Once, while walking near the Peter Pan statue in Kensington Gardens, I noticed another small boy with bandaged knees. I turned to the current nannie and asked why this was so. She replied sternly that the boy had eaten too many sweets; so many that they had bred worms in his inside, which were now wriggling out through holes they had bored in his legs. It sounds ridiculous now, but this and similar remarks had the effect of putting me off most forms of food for many years; I refused to eat meat, screamed loudly at the sight of a fish-monger's slab, and once fainted from sheer hunger in a lift at Marshall & Snelgrove's. The doctor said I must be a 'natural vegetarian'. Of course I did not tell my parents that I was afraid of being devoured by worms, and my lack of appetite must

14

have given them considerable anxiety. Even now, I do not care for sweets.

There were all kinds of childish fears. Worst of all was my fear of the dark. I used to lie awake with a thumping heart, trying not to look at the shadows cast by the night-light on the walls. All the things that had upset and fascinated me during the daytime came crowding back into my imagination at those times. In the winter there was a tall, old-fashioned oil stove in my nursery, with a top pierced with little holes through which the light shone on to the ceiling. This pattern of light, so steady and comforting, became for me a symbol of Good, driving out the evil influence of the writhing shadows on the wall. On nights when the stove was not lit, I used to hide my head under the bedclothes and repeat, over and over again, the only prayer I knew: 'Gentle Jesus, meek and mild, look upon a little child, pity my simplicity, suffer me to come to Thee' – an incantation which seemed, even then, pitifully inadequate against the demons which were crouching in the corners.

Far more comforting than Jesus were Winnie-the-Pooh, Tigger, Eeyore, and a Kanga made of white stockingette, with a matching Roo in her pouch. These all shared my bed and watched over me, their boot-button eyes fixed in unwinking stares on all the corners of the nursery in case some nameless Thing should leap out of the shadows. Grown-ups may laugh, but thousands of children are probably taking the same precautions to-night.

When I was about five I began to attend a kindergarten in Earl's Court, where I made a few friends and discovered that there was one place in the world even more terrifying than my nursery. This was the Bolivian Embassy, where I went to my first party. Everything began well, with a stupendous tea which culminated in the presentation, to each child, of a wooden box of crystallized plums. In the delight and confusion provoked by this largesse I wandered away, clutching my box of plums, through a curtained doorway and down a dark corridor. At the end of this, in an illuminated niche, stood a carving of a woman's head – presumably a Spanish madonna – gilded and painted, with pink lips and a crystal tear oozing from each closed eye. Convinced that the head was real and freshly severed, I uttered a shocked howl which brought all the servants running. I was not invited to the Embassy again.

It was the ambition of all parents at this time – and mine were no exception – to send their children to a good school. This meant one which would give them certain clear social advantages in later life, teach them the gentlemanly sports and the rudiments of education, and, most important of all, give them the cachet of 'leadership' which most families above a certain level of income believed, in 1930, to be the birthright of their sons. This was mainly a question of speaking BBC English, cultivating a quiet taste in dress, using the right knife and fork and avoiding, like the plague, any interest or accomplishment which might set one apart from all the other little boys who were being put through the same mill.

It must be extremely difficult for parents, assisted only by flattering brochures and the advice of friends, to choose a preparatory school for their sons, and perhaps in the end it makes little difference which one they select. I was sent to school as a boarder at the age of seven and remained there until I moved on to a public school seven years later. It may have been no worse than many other schools, but its effect on me was deplorable. Incessant bullying induced in me a painful shyness which took years to overcome, and when I took refuge in friendship with other outcasts like myself we were publicly ridiculed by the masters, who used to observe that 'Sops of a feather flock together'. Sops, of course, were boys incapable of bringing glory to the school on football-ground or cricket-pitch; the persecution only succeeded in drawing them closer together, until they formed a kind of secret society – a childish underworld tragically like that of sexual inverts.

I suppose I must always have known that I was different from other children, but it took me years to find out in what way I differed. Even then I was attracted to my own sex, long before I knew what sex was about; but this seemed perfectly natural, since the only people who showed any kindness to me were the other boys who were also looked down upon by the rest. The masters frightened me. There were – as I found out much later – several homosexuals among them, but these were not the ones who did most harm. It was the aggressively virile

16

type of teacher, always trying to mould the boys into his own tough pattern, who first made me feel that I was a failure and an outcast.

All games were compulsory, but it was usually possible to get through them without too much derision, provided that one ran about a good deal without actually getting in the way of the experts. The exception was boxing. This took place in the evenings and was presided over by a master who selected the contestants himself. I might have made a fairly adequate boxer if my nose had not bled so easily, and I am sure it would have done my nine-year-old ego a great deal of good if I had been allowed to fight, and perhaps beat, one of the other boys who made my life so unpleasant. This, however, was not the master's plan. It was his habit, with a kind of gloating relish, to arrange for those whom he considered 'Sops' to fight each other; so that I would find myself, covered in blood, lunging painfully at the only other boy in the school whom I really liked, while the master danced around yelling 'Come on, no kitten-pats!'.

I was, at this time, a remarkably unattractive child, exceedingly thin and clumsy, with spots and a mop of carroty hair. Once when another boy's parents, arriving in a Rolls-Royce, had narrowly missed me as I blundered out of the front door, I heard the mother exclaim: 'Who was that hideous small boy we nearly ran over?' I did not expect to be liked, and only wished to be inconspicuous; but this did not seem possible. I eventually discovered, however, that there was one thing I could do which pleased the masters, if not the other boys: I could be a 'swot'. Obtaining a scholarship to another school was grudgingly conceded to be almost as good as getting into the First Eleven, and this I set myself to do.

Another way in which I could escape some of the miseries of school, I discovered, was by being ill. It was possible, if suspected of having some contagious ailment, to achieve a little peace and quiet and even some sympathy by being confined, 'under observation', in Matron's sitting-room. Constitutionally I am quite strong, but during this period I succeeded in catching all the usual diseases and was able to produce a streaming cold or a fainting fit whenever some particularly undesirable event was in the offing. Curiously enough, this habit has persisted ever since; my only illnesses occur, like involuntary alibis, at moments of mental stress.

We were forced, every Sunday, to sit down in the Big Schoolroom and write letters to our parents. Since these were afterwards read through by the master on duty – ostensibly to see if they were long enough – it is not surprising that they failed to convey my real feelings about the school. Several times during the term our mothers and fathers were permitted to come and take us out for the day. On these occasions the staff positively radiated wholesome charm and any signs of misery were ascribed by our parents to a perfectly natural longing for home. It is extraordinary to what lengths children will go to conceal their inner feelings from their parents; I am sure that mine never suspected how unhappy I was.

All this time I was growing up, although nobody attempted to explain the process to me. Biological details were, of course, frequently discussed by the boys in a wildly inaccurate manner, the whole subject of sex being generally described as 'dirt', 'smut' or 'piggishness' by the pupils, and by the masters whenever it came to their notice. The idea that the changes now taking place in our bodies were in any way connected with the production of children, let alone with love between men and women, remarkably enough never occurred to us. Sex was something isolated, furtive, and unclean, like going to the lavatory – only worse. It was only much later, just before I left the school, that the headmaster drew me aside and imparted the information which any working-class child would have acquired years before.

The happiest times of my childhood were usually solitary ones. When I was ten we went to live in the country, in a rambling oak-beamed farmhouse on the edge of a forest. This was – and still is – an enchanted place to me. As a lonely child, I led a dream life there to which hardly anyone was admitted. At the back of the house there were fields sloping down to a stream, on the other side of which the forest began. Sometimes on summer days, when the stream was trickling sluggishly, I jumped across to the far bank where clumps of reed-mace and wild mint grew. Moorhens and water-rats scurried away at my approach. I never stayed there long, although the water was full of interesting creatures, sticklebacks and water boatmen and caddis grubs encased in ramshackle home-made houses. My objective was the forest, beyond the screen of alder bushes that wept over the stream, their blue-black twigs whispering in the current.

My favourite books, at this time, were *The Swiss Family Robinson*, *The Coral Island*, and *The Jungle Book*. There was nothing tropical, however, about my own Sussex forest except in my imagination, where I could make what I liked of it. The hidden marsh where the kingcups lifted their gold heads became a mangrove swamp buzzing with deadly mosquitoes. The slender ropes of ivy and honeysuckle that trailed from the bushes were transformed into strong lianas, on which a man might swing away from the horn of a charging rhinoceros; the wood pigeons were dazzling macaws and lyre-birds, and at any moment a leopard might step delicately through the bluebells and the bracken.

When I walked away from the house and across the fields, I usually took a trowel or a butterfly-net in order to give an apparent purpose to the expedition. If anyone asked what I had been doing when I returned I could always say that I had been chasing moths or tadpoles, or looking for the rare pin-cushions of moss which had been kicked up by horses and grown green and quilted on both sides. This was partly true, but my main purpose in going to the forest was to escape. Even in the winter, it was better than anywhere else. The trees were bare and the ground hard with frost, but there were still treasures to be found, holly trees and mountain ash all afire with berries, badgers' tracks in the snow and the mysterious spindle tree with its coral-coloured seeds. Deep in the forest there were even stranger things; once there had been a private zoo there, and sometimes in a clearing a family of wallabies could be seen, crouching in the grass like enormous hares.

Every summer we used to spend a week or two at my grand-father's house at Winchelsea; a different landscape, but one which also belonged to me. Here, everything was open to the winds and the clouds, and the little town rose out of the surrounding marshes like a ship with a thousand years of history for its cargo. Every time you dug a hole in Winchelsea, your spade turned up fragments of the past, and I used to hover round the Council workmen to examine what they found – thick Georgian pennies, pieces of iridescent glass, clay pipe-stems, Saxon groats, and Victorian money-tokens. Once they brought me a coin of bronze, as big as a half-crown, which they had found in a place called Dead Man's Lane. The name and profile of Antoninus Pius, Emperor of Rome, were clearly stamped on it. For the first time, the past became for me as real as the present day. It was the first time, too, I think, that I realized the true value of learning. Because I had decided to win a scholarship, I had devoured Greek, Latin, and History with a parrot-like, stupid glibness; now, confronted by this antique profile of a dead king, I passionately desired knowledge for its own sake.

I won the scholarship when I was thirteen, and went to my public school. So far, I had learned several things. Firstly, the greatest possible virtue was to be exactly like everybody else. Secondly, through some curious disability or difference which was probably my fault, I was unfitted for the role expected of me. Thirdly, I could escape from the real world of competition and failure into an invisible world of my own, which, if I worked hard enough, I could share with all the other men and women, living and dead, who had bequeathed their wisdom and imagination for people like me to dig up, like coins in a ditch.

I cannot remember much about my first year at public school, except that the discipline was very strict and that there were hundreds of rules for new boys to memorize; not only school rules of a necessary kind, but a mass of bewildering regulations laid down by the prefects, which we all had to learn by heart. There was some rule, which I now forget, about the number of jacket buttons which a boy of any given age was allowed to leave undone, and there were all kinds of privileges – such as walking across certain patches of lawn – which belonged only to senior boys and must not be infringed. These were intended to impart an air of tradition and antiquity to the establishment, which had actually been founded in the reign of Queen Victoria.

We wore gowns in class, and white surplices and mortar-boards in chapel. I do not know what gave me the idea that I was musical, but I joined the choir and learned to play the trumpet and the bugle. One advantage of this was that it made it possible to join the OTC band and practise in the music-rooms while the rest of the cadets were doing rifle drill. Games were, of course, compulsory, but there was a much wider choice than there had been at my preparatory school – rugby, soccer, hockey, rowing, swimming, cricket, and athletics. There was also more variety in the subjects taught, and a teaching staff which included several men with a really brilliant flair for arousing their pupils' interest. They en-couraged me in my belief that learning, instead of being a drudgery and a bore, could be an exciting experience with unlimited rewards, and I shall always be grateful to them. I realized, later, that they, too, must have been grateful when they found a boy who was willing to listen to them; so many of their pupils were quite incapable of profiting by the expensive education which their parents were paying for.

There was a wonderful library at the school, and that was where I spent most of my time, sitting at a table in one of the quiet, book-lined bays, forgetting everything outside the circle of light shining on the page before me. I devoured books as other boys devoured crumpets in the tuck-shop, rushing through novels, plays, criticism, poetry, and history as though I only had an hour to live and must know everything before I died. Some of my reading was suggested to me by masters; some of it was the chance result of my continuous, headlong treasure-hunt among the shelves, and I must have consumed a good deal of dross along with the gold. I have never been able, in later years, to read with such concentration or such speed, but by the time I left school I was crammed with the richness of print and have been digesting it, slowly, ever since.

One of the immediate results was that I became at the same time intensely romantic and very, very cynical – a strange and, indeed, impossible combination. My hero at the moment was Shelley, with his incandescent vision of beauty and his dis-astrous effect on those who loved him. I went on wanting to be like Shelley until I discovered that Mr Aldous Huxley, another of my heroes, had described him as 'a fat white fairy slug'.

By the time I had read the whole of Shakespeare, Emily Brontë, and Baudelaire I knew all about love, or imagined that I did – but I still knew very little about sex. Indeed, I hardly connected the two. Love was a soaring emotion which people died for; Sex was something to be discussed in whispers. My housemaster had warned us in an end-of-term speech to beware of 'smoking, drinking, and sordid sexual adventures', but I did not know why. It turned out later that two of the senior boys had been discovered experimenting together in the boiler-house; but, generally speaking, the school was fairly free from this kind of behaviour. There were, of course, many strong emotional friendships between boys which probably had an unconsciously homosexual basis – this happens in every school and it seems to do no permanent harm.

The sexual feelings of 'teen-age' boys are very much stronger than most adults care to admit. Some biologists, in fact, suggest that they are stronger at this period than at any other. It is not, therefore, very sensible to confine a boy, between the ages of fourteen and eighteen, to an all-male boarding school. The first stirrings of sex in childhood, we are told, are directed indiscriminately towards all kinds of objects and persons; it is during adolescence that they are – or should be – orientated towards the opposite sex. In co-educational schools or in large families this may be an easy transition; and the great majority of boys, even at public schools, are of course able to make it. They are the lucky ones. Others, like myself, find themselves with strong sexual feelings which not only have no possible physical outlet, but no objective to which they may be directed; and the quest for such an objective – for a person, in fact, to love – leads in many cases to homo-sexuality.

It was at this stage that the pattern of my future emotional life began to develop. I was lonely and shy, so I looked for a friend with whom I could share any happiness that came my way. Secretly ashamed of my failure to compete with other boys in sports and feats of strength, I needed the friendship of someone who possessed the qualities which I myself lacked; somebody strong and self-confident and brave. Since my success in the class-room was the only accomplishment of which I felt I could be proud, I did not want anyone who would overshadow it. The companion I sought, in fact, was somebody who would outshine me physically but not intellectually; he would be the body, I would be the brain. The approach, of course, was not as cold-blooded as this and I do not suppose that I had much conscious idea of what I was looking for; but that, I can see now, was the pattern of my search.

There were plenty of boys who fitted the description. I used to watch them rowing on the river, handsome, muscular and slightly dim, as unapproachable as gods. I would run to hold their boats as they embarked, hoping that one of them would speak to me. But it was quite impossible. Most of them were a year or two older than myself and boys of different ages simply did not speak to each other. It was not done. It was against all the rules which I had had to learn by heart during my first term. Between us, there was a gulf as wide and deep as that between a Brahmin and an Untouchable. Solitary and hopeless, I burrowed even deeper into my books.

From them, I learned something which I had not even suspected before. I forget now which book it was that first gave a meaning to the half-conscious quest which I had been vainly pursuing; Plato, I suppose, or Proust, or some commentary on Shakespeare's sonnets. There were men, I discovered, who only loved other men. This did not strike me as strange; indeed, it seemed perfectly reasonable. The physical perfection of an athlete had always appeared to me more beautiful than the body of a woman, and a man's mind more flexible and strong; only a man could give me that feeling of protection against an unfriendly world for which I longed. Love, for me, meant comradeship, and I could not imagine a relationship of that kind with a woman. I wanted someone who would make me brave, and whom I would make wise. A sentence in Plato's Symposium haunted me: 'An army of such lovers could conquer the world'.

*

This was in 1941. Leaving school at eighteen, I had won a scholarship to Oxford, and at first I intended to go there for a

23

year before I went to war. Many of my friends were already in the Army; my cousin, a Spitfire pilot in the RAF, had been killed a year before during the Battle of Britain. I had known Oxford well, since it was near my school, but now the heart seemed to have gone out of it. I stayed in my College for ten days, becoming more and more discontented. Finally, I became ill. I left Oxford and decided not to go back until the war was over, forfeiting my Service deferment and waiting to be called up. My doctor sent me to a heart specialist, who reported I needed a rest and should on no account enter the Services just yet. He gave me a letter to give to the Medical Board to which I was due to be called.

Instead of delivering the letter, I volunteered for aircrew duties in the RAF and was immediately accepted. The first 'camp' to which I was drafted consisted of several blocks of flats in St John's Wood, containing a large number of young men of my own age; but age was all we had in common. There were a few public schoolboys, but the majority were working men, many of whom had started to earn their own living at a time when I was still cooking kippers on the prefects' gas ring and learning German verbs. Years before, at my preparatory school, one of the masters had remarked that it was only by the merest chance that boys like me were enjoying the advantages of education, and that there were probably many gardeners' boys who would be better equipped to profit by it. I remembered this now. The RAF was a new and mysterious world, full of new rules which had to be learned again from the beginning. The enormous amount of information which I had crammed into my head during the last eleven years seemed, at first, quite useless. I was an extremely raw recruit, always doing the wrong thing. Having spent most of my time in the Officers' Training Corps at school playing the bugle, I was atrociously clumsy at drill. The corporals bawled at me. My uniform did not fit. I was totally unable to recognize aircraft by their silhouettes. My boots pinched. Morse was a closed book to me. But for the first time in my life away from home, I was enjoying every minute of it.

Instead of looking down on me for my incompetence, as my fellow-pupils at school would have done, the other cadets set themselves to encourage and help me. They taught me how to shine my boots with a hot spoon and a piece of orange-peel, and how to smoke a cigarette without attracting the flight sergeant's attention. If we were marching along with a pile of kit in our arms and I dropped the whole lot in the road, they picked it up and carried it for me. They laughed at my public school accent and taught me to speak Cockney. They showed me how to conceal my knife, fork and spoon inside my gas-mask case, so that I was always able to get into the head of the mess-queue. I made friends with a Scots grocer's boy, a customs clerk from Plumstead and an ex-burglar whose normal method of re-entry to the billet was by way of a piece of rope which we left dangling from the window.

We went to Southern Rhodesia for our flying training. It was a strange land in which to begin one's adult life; a vast, hot and ugly country which seemed to tolerate its inhabitants, black and white, merely as an elephant tolerates flies. From the air, it was almost impossible to see any traces of civilization. At ground-level, however, there was a good deal of scurrying about, with endless sundowner-parties to mitigate the boredom of the place. The RAF 'other ranks' were viewed with a certain amount of suspicion, but through introductions from friends I was able to meet a number of charming and hospitable people. I learned to fly solo, but it became clear eventually that I was, in the words of my instructor, temperamentally unsuited to war-time flying. I had a curious and expensive habit of landing my Tiger Moth on its tail, somewhat in the manner of a mallard alighting on water. After I had bent several tail-skids flush with the fuselage in a forward direction, I was advised to re-muster to the ground staff.

There was only a limited choice: I could become either a cook and butcher, a meteorologist, or a pigeon keeper in the Signals. Although physics had always been my worst subject at school, I decided to be a meteorologist, since this would give me opportunities to see some of the wilder parts of Northern Rhodesia, where there was a chain of airfields linking South Africa to the Middle East. I spent the next three years in this way, usually living in a thatched mud hut in some inaccessible place. I acquired a handsome moustache, a pet cheetah and a monkey named Sinatra, a quantity of leopard skins and the title of Shinganga wa Mfula, Wizard of the Rain, which was bestowed on me by a local witch-doctor.

No magic powers, however, were needed in order to forecast the Rhodesian weather, which consisted of blazing sunshine for nine months in the year and pouring rain for the remaining three. I spent most of my time loafing about with an ancient 12-bore shotgun, or making pencil sketches of the natives. Sometimes I wondered what I would do after the war was ended. The masters at school had always prophesied that I would become a writer, but so far I had written nothing but halting little poems and a few plays based on such colourful incidents as the destruction of Pompeii and the opening of Tutankhamen's tomb, with a tendency towards melodrama and blank verse.

Northern Rhodesia was not a place in which to make plans for the future. It was quite impossible, surrounded by glittering rocks and twisted thorn-trees, the coughing of leopards and the honking of hornbills, to visualize crowded London and the necessity of earning one's living. And then, suddenly, the war was over. Because I held a scholarship to a university, I was eligible for an immediate release, and by November, 1945, I was back at Oxford – one of a crowd of ex-servicemen trying to accustom themselves to the idea of being back at school.

*

During the war years I had had a number of experiences with women, but none with men. I still hoped that one day I should meet a girl whom I could love and eventually marry, but my relationships in Rhodesia were physical and brief; there always seemed to be something lacking. I was already beginning to think of myself as a homosexual, but it was as yet only an emotional bias, with no physical expression.

It is often claimed that the greatest danger to the community from homosexuals comes from their tendency to make 'converts', continually drawing into their circle young men who, if they were left alone, would grow up perfectly normal. It is further said that 90 per cent of homosexual cases known to psychiatrists start with seduction. From my own experience, I would say that neither of these statements is true.

I have already said that many boys at my school indulged in homosexual practices without, apparently, growing up into homosexuals. I believe that such experiences would only have a permanent effect if the tendencies were already present in the boy, as they were in my case. It does not seem reasonable to allege – as is so often done when a schoolmaster appears in the dock – that a child can be permanently diverted into homosexuality by a single experience of this kind.

There were several homosexual masters at both my schools, as I later discovered, but they are the last people whom I would blame for my condition. They never made any attempt to seduce me. The damage was not done by them, but by the 'normal' masters – or those with violently suppressed homosexual desires – who either did not understand what was the matter with me, or else recognized it only too clearly as something which existed, also, in themselves. Later on, I discovered that such people were the worst enemies of the homosexual. A normally-adjusted man is surprisingly tolerant; the scorn and the denunciations nearly always come from a man with more or less suppressed homosexual desires of his own. This phenomenon is known to psychologists as 'projection'; when a man is ashamed of something in his own nature, he relieves himself of his guilt by strenuously denouncing it in other people. Mr Gordon Westwood, in his well-documented and enlightened study *Society and the Homosexual* (Gollancz, 1952) says:

A tendency towards alcoholism may be replaced by a fanatical attitude towards temperance; the desire to excel at games and the awareness of some physical disability may be closely allied in origin; a talkative and bombastic disposition may hide a gnawing feeling of inferiority in the unconscious; and an aggressive, vitriolic attitude to homosexuality may be a defence against these tendencies.

Due to early influences beyond their control, hundreds of thousands of men have marked homosexual tendencies in their make-up. The violence of their denunciation represents a desperate repudiation of their own homosexual tendencies. It is impossible for these people to approach the problem of homosexuality with any kind of emotional detachment. Many of these people are as badly in need of psychological treatment as the homosexuals they so violently condemn.

Towards the end of my schooldays and during the first few months of my service in the RAF, I had met a number of people connected in various ways with the theatre and other arts, some of whom were frankly homosexual. The fact was openly discussed, and it must have been obvious to them that although I already had a bias in that direction, I was entirely inexperienced; but, instead of taking advantage of my inexperience, as some people might think they would be tempted to do, they left me severely alone. The ability of men of this kind to behave in a way which, in any other context, would be described as 'moral', is by no means unusual, but it is often forgotten in the heat of discussion.

At Oxford I met a great many people. This was, in fact, the main purpose of going back to the university, as I saw it. I added another scholarship to the one which I already held, but after this there seemed little point in acquiring further academic honours. I did as little work as possible, but I made hundreds of friends. The undergraduate population at that time was of an unusual kind, consisting in about equal proportions of young men who had come straight from school and others who had served in the forces, many of whom had wives and families. We did not pay much attention to the regulations; the ex-servicemen did not take kindly to the ban on public houses and ignored the midnight curfew, returning to their colleges in the early hours of the morning by scaling walls and squeezing through gaps in railings. As one of them said, we had all been either bored to death or frightened to death during the war, and we did not propose to waste any more time. There were parties every night; theatre parties, bump-supper parties, sherry parties, and week-end parties in London. Even the lady don responsible for my studies produced a bottle of Pernod with which to enliven our discussions on medieval lyrics.

I met a man with whom I had been at school. He had been a naval officer, with some staff appointment in Ceylon. He said that most of the officers at the station had been 'gay', and looked at me as though this was some password to which he expected me to reply. I had not heard the expression before, but apparently it was an American euphemism for homosexual. He was, of course, gay himself, and took it for granted that I was, too. I was surprised and rather impressed. He did not look in the least like the popular idea of homosexual, being well-built, masculine, and neatly dressed. This was something new to me. Although I was perfectly prepared to admit that love could exist between men, I had always been slightly repelled by the obvious homosexuals whom I had met because of their vanity, their affected manner, and their ceaseless chatter. These, it now appeared, formed only a small part of the homosexual world, although the most noticeable one – the exposed ninth, so to speak, of a very large iceberg.

The number of homosexuals in England and Wales has never been satisfactorily estimated. Some statisticians have given a figure of 150,000; others, of over a million. If the Kinsey report, based on inquiries in America, is accepted as a rough indication, the figure for England and Wales can be estimated at 650,000. This refers only to men who are exclusively homosexual; Kinsey found that in the USA more than a third of the entire male population had some homosexual experience between adolescence and old age.

It is, of course, perfectly obvious that only a very small proportion of this 650,000 is noticeably odd. It is equally evident that homosexuality is not, as some propagandists would have us believe, a kind of fashionable vice restricted to decadent intellectuals and degenerate clergymen. This idea is extremely useful to those who wish to influence public opinion against homosexuality, and it succeeds because the British people, on the whole, despise intellectuals and distrust the clergy. But it does not happen to be correct. In a recent survey of 321 court cases involving homosexuality, it was found that the accused men fell into the following categories:

Shop and clerical workers	16%
Artisan (factory workers)	15%
Transport and Post Office	11%
Unskilled labourers	10%

Armed forces	10%
Hotel and domestic servants	7%
Students, trainees, schoolboys	6%
Schoolmasters	4%
Agricultural workers	4%
Clergymen	2%
Mentally deficient	2%
Independent means	2%
Unclassified	11%

Homosexuals are a minority, and are persecuted as such. They do not, however, form a cohesive or organized group, as other minorities do. For the most part they are isolated, not only from the rest of the community, but from each other. The fear under which they live creates no freemasonry among them; the problem of homosexuality is not the problem of a group, but of hundreds of thousands of individuals – each of whom, according to the laws of Britain, is a criminal.

If all the homosexuals in this country were to be rounded up and imprisoned, they would fill the existing gaols thirty times over.

*

But in 1946 I was not concerned with statistics; I merely wanted to lead my own life. I knew, of course, that homosexual conduct was illegal; but so were many other things which everyone did at that time, like trading in clothing coupons and buying eggs on the black market. Furthermore, it hardly seemed likely that the existing laws, antique and savage as they might be, would ever be used against men who were living, according to their lights, in a moral and discreet manner. I know that the word 'moral' may sound out of place in this context, but it seemed to me then – and it still does – that there are different degrees of morality (or immorality, if you like) in relationships between men, just as there are in relationships between men and women. At one time adultery and fornication were crimes, as homosexuality is to-day. The essence of a crime, presumably, is the fact that some harm is done to someone. But who does the most harm? The adulterer, stealing a man's wife, breaking up a home and perhaps affecting the

30

whole course of her children's lives? The man who seduces a girl and abandons her with an illegitimate child? Or two men who prefer to live together?

Earlier generations may have tried to ignore such questions. During the first years of peace, after a war fought, according to our rulers, for four indispensable freedoms, they were widely discussed by all kinds of people, men and women, normal as well as homosexual. It was even being responsibly suggested, for the first time, that the laws of Britain should be brought into line with those of other countries, where sexual conduct in private between consenting adult males was not considered a crime. But most of us were not interested in law reform and hardly gave a thought to the possibility of prosecution. We always supposed – and the cases reported in the newspapers appeared to bear this out – that if we behaved ourselves in public, the police would leave us alone.

I say 'us', because by this time I had become accustomed to thinking of myself as a homosexual. It was partly a social attitude. I had always been irritated and distressed by the rigidity of the English class system, even though I had derived every possible benefit from it myself. Thanks to my scholarships, I had received a 'good education' and would therefore presumably be in a position to walk with kings if ever the opportunity arose, but it seemed more difficult to retain the common touch. I instinctively rebelled against a system by which a man, whatever his personal qualities might be, was indelibly labelled 'Top Drawer', 'Middle Drawer', or 'Bottom Drawer', merely by the manner in which he spoke. Having served for four years in the ranks of the RAF, I had met many working men and was proud to call them my friends. Now that the war for freedom was over, I was no longer supposed to speak to them, because they were not 'my class'. The social rules seemed to me as ridiculous as those imitation traditions which I had had to learn at school.

The homosexual world knows no such boundaries – which is precisely why it is so much hated and feared by many of our political diehards. The real crime of Lord Montagu, for example, in the eyes of some 'Society' people, was that he became acquainted – on no matter what basis – with a man who (to quote the prosecuting counsel) was 'infinitely his social inferior'.

I do not believe that anyone is 'infinitely the social inferior' of anyone else. People are either pleasant or unpleasant, entertaining or tedious, trustworthy or dishonest, and these qualities are in no way related to accidents of birth. There are plenty of boring Earls and brilliant bricklayers and there are also delightful Dukes and deplorable dustmen; one should at least be allowed the freedom to choose one's friends.

I shall probably be accused of letting my sexual preferences colour my social views; it will be said that my fondness for working people is due not so much to their excellences of character as to their physical attractiveness. There may be some truth in this, but I can only say that if homosexuality results in a heightened awareness of social injustice, it is – in this way, if in no other – a force for good.

As it happens, the person of whom I was most fond at this period was a foreign prince, whom I had met during one of my frequent week-ends in London. He was extremely intelligent, considerate and kind, and I would not dream of embarrassing him by giving any clues to his identity. He knew everybody in London, it seemed, both in the homosexual world and out of it, from Cabinet ministers to the proprietress of a Mayfair brothel with whom we used to take afternoon tea. She had navy-blue false eyelashes and I remember her telling us how she had stolen her bedroom carpet, which was almond pink, from the ladies' toilet at Ciro's by wrapping it round her and pretending it was an evening cloak.

For the first time I began to understand how the word 'gay' had come to mean what it did. So many people have written about homosexuality in a spirit of self-pity and shame that I feel bound to confess that I thoroughly enjoyed my adventure with the prince. He was a delightful companion, and though we quarrelled frequently it never lasted very long. When I parted from him, finally, it was because I imagined that I had fallen in love with a woman.

I was 24 and on the point of leaving Oxford, although I still had no idea of what my career should be. My woman friend was five years older, a sweet and sympathetic person who knew many of my 'gay' companions and had no illusions about me. Neither of us thought it would matter. We talked of marriage and of having a family. Everything seemed perfect. I passed my Finals at Oxford with Second Class Honours – better than I deserved, considering how little work I had done. And then everything became gloomy and impossible again, as though the sun had withdrawn behind a cloud.

*

I had no money, no job, and no prospects. My university degree qualified me for nothing except teaching, which did not appeal to me. Ex-servicemen were a drug on the market. I tramped round the BBC, the film studios, and the publishing houses. It was the same everywhere: nobody would give me a job until I had some experience, and the only way of acquiring experience was by getting a job. 'I shouldn't bank on a job in television, old man; it's an overcrowded profession, you know.' 'I tell you what – why don't you go away and write something, then we can have a look at it.' 'So many qualified journalists coming back from the war just now, it's pretty hopeless for a beginner.' 'My friend has a friend who used to know Sir Alexander Korda, but I think he's in New York.' 'No, I'm afraid it isn't the kind of thing we want.' The Editor regrets ... the Editor regrets.

I took a job as a waiter in a small residential hotel at £5 a week. I had to get up at dawn to stoke the boilers, help to cook the breakfasts and sweep the dining-room, as well as waiting at table. At night, I wrote. I sold an article to *Vogue*, one to *Printer's Pie* and two to *Punch*. Then I got the sack for arguing with the proprietress. I went home to my parents and wrote a play about Northern Rhodesia. It was a farce about the groundnuts scheme, called *Primrose and the Peanuts*. It was performed one Sunday evening at the Playhouse Theatre and later, for two weeks, with a different cast, at the Bedford Theatre in Camden Town, which was then being used for 'try-outs' with a view to production in the West End. It received excellent reviews in the *Observer*, the *Evening News* and the *New Statesman*, and Sir Beverley Baxter in the *Evening Standard* was kind enough to say that the third act was 'pure Shaw'. They all agreed that it should be transferred to Shaftesbury Avenue, but the theatre managements demurred; they said that the groundnuts scheme was a dated subject which would not 'draw them in'. I was left with an exercise-book full of Press cuttings and a net profit of £200.

In the meantime I had joined the *Daily Mail* as a reporter, starting in the district office at Leeds at a salary of £6 a week. I lodged in a council house at Meanwood and spent most of the time ringing up the local police, ambulance, and fire stations to see if there was any 'news'. Occasionally I stumbled on some item which could be given an unusual twist, but most of the stories fell into clearly-defined categories. There was the one which began: 'A little grey-haired woman sat last night wondering . . . ' And: 'Everybody in Heckmondwike knows Jock, the lovable shaggy-haired Scottie. . . . ' And: 'This is the story of a little girl who wanted to be a nun . . . ' And: 'Police of four counties were last night searching for . . . ' All human experience, I discovered, could be reduced to some formula of this sort; and the more closely one stuck to the formula, the higher one's stock rose at the main office.

One day I was sent to cover the British Medical Association's annual conference at Harrogate, an unpromising assignment which I faithfully translated into terms of 'a tiny grey-haired woman doctor who, etc.' As the lady had been making some criticism of the National Health Scheme, to which the *Daily Mail* was opposed, the story achieved the distinction of appearing on the front page as the main news item in all editions, under a seven-column headline: 'BMA IN NEW REVOLT'. I took the first morning train to London, ran the Editor to earth in a pub, and persuaded him that it was time for me to deploy my talents in Fleet Street.

During the next five years I was successively general reporter, gossip columnist, Festival of Britain correspondent, assistant dramatic critic, Buckingham Palace reporter, Coronation columnist and Diplomatic correspondent. I attended the fabulous fancy-dress ball given by Charles de Beistegui in Venice and covered the Craig and Bentley shooting at Croydon; I dug up the facts of Haigh's early life and reported the progress of King Farouk's honeymoon tour; I interviewed Tallulah Bankhead and the Crown Prince of Tonga and the mother of Mate Dancy of the *Flying Enterprise*; I went to Royal garden-parties and waded through the East Coast floods; I chased the Missing Diplomats as far as the South of France, and saw Queen Mary's funeral, and nearly got the sack for being disrespectful about Gilbert and Sullivan; I spent 14 hours in a small French fishing-boat off the Cherbourg coast looking for a sunken submarine and returned to Southampton, black with diesel-oil and smelling strongly of fish, in a first-class cabin on the *Queen Mary*.

Fleet Street men are always amused when people come up to them at parties and gush: 'What a wonderful time you reporters must have, going to all those places and meeting such interesting people!' The truth is that a reporter's life is about as satisfactory as a film-programme would be if it were made up entirely of 'trailers'. Eventually, he despairs of ever finding out the truth about anything, because he never has time. There is always an edition to catch. Everything, on a national morning newspaper, has to be written from a frenzied 'last night angle'; it is apparently of no interest to the waiting millions to learn that a little grey-haired mother sat weeping last Tuesday; it is necessary that she should weep last night. Furthermore, the things that she is permitted to weep about are clearly defined. People sometimes complain about the hackneyed phrases in which newspaper stories are written, but nobody ever seems to notice the hackneyed laws of What Is News which inexorably govern them. Anything fresh, strange, or unexpected is rigidly excluded, in spite of Lord Northcliffe's memorable dictum about 'man bites dog'. If this story ever appears on the front page, it will probably be in terms of a film-star's ex-husband taking a bite out of a lovable, shaggy-haired Scottie.

If reporters are over-conventional in their writing, they are no less so in their way of life. Fleet Street, in spite of one or two flamboyant and rather self-conscious exceptions, is not in the smallest degree Bohemian. It is a hard-working, nervous community with shabby suits and nicotine-stained fingers, living on beer and sandwiches and catching the last train home to the suburbs. Its contacts with the great, wide, lurid world about which it writes are usually brief, disenchanting and fraught with suspicion on both sides. At one moment a reporter may be trying to gate-crash an Earl's wedding in a hired morning-coat; an hour later he is in Stepney, persuading a group of stevedores that, at heart, he is one of them. Both worlds are equally hostile and he is at home in neither, but he returns to the office, lights another cigarette and, like a quick-change artist, obediently assumes the respective points of view which are expected of him: 'Detectives yesterday mingled with the guests at the fabulous, £20,000 reception after the St Margaret's, Westminster, S.W., wedding of the popular Earl of . . .' and, a few minutes later: 'Everybody in Cable-street, E., knows Charlie, the veteran organizer of the Amalgamated Society of Pushers and Heavers. . . .'

Fortunately for them, most of the reporters I knew were not frustrated writers swimming against the tide; they were workmen who happened to use words instead of nuts and bolts or bricks. I liked them very much. The people whom I did not like were the men at the top, a cold-eyed bunch of businessmen who peddled tragedy, sensation, and heartbreak as casually as though they were cartloads of cabbages or bags of cement. The false, over-coloured and sentimental view of life reflected in the newspapers was due to the cynical belief of these men that this was what the public wanted.

Later, I became a subject for newspaper headlines myself. From the peculiar vantage-point of someone who has been both hunter and hunted, I can look back on Fleet Street with amusement, but without anger. When it was necessary for reporters to interview me, I found nothing to complain of in their individual behaviour. I think the stories which people tell of being 'harried by the Press' are probably exaggerated. The reporter always gets the blame, but the real culprits are the proprietors and editors who relentlessly pursue the trivial and the sordid, while protesting that they are shocked by what they have to print.

I could hardly have chosen a profession in which being a homosexual was more of a handicap than it was in Fleet Street. Its morality was that of the saloon bar: every sexual excess was talked about and tolerated, provided it was 'normal'. It has always seemed strange to me that a man's popularity should so often depend on the extent to which he boasts of his seductions and adulteries, as though promiscuity and deceitfulness were the certificates of manhood, and I used to imagine the shocked amazement of all these 'broad-minded' people if I were to tell them the truth about myself.

I was forced to be deceitful, living one life during my working hours and another when I was free. I had two sets of friends; almost, one might say, two faces. At the back of my mind there was always a nagging fear that my two worlds might suddenly collide; that somebody who knew about me would meet somebody who did not know, and that disaster would ensue. I was quite clear about what I meant by 'disaster'. I did not want to be exposed as a homosexual, not only because exposure might lead to prosecution and imprisonment, but because I knew that it would cause the greatest humiliation to my family.

I had, on several occasions, discussed the problems of homosexuality, in general terms, with my mother and father, hoping to find some way of telling them about myself. But it was impossible. Their attitude, like that of so many people, was not one of particular condemnation or of particular tolerance; it was simply that they had not given the matter much thought, because they did not believe that they knew any homosexuals.

The strain of deceiving my family and friends often became intolerable. It was necessary for me to watch every word I spoke, and every gesture that I made, in case I gave myself away. When jokes were made about 'queers' I had to laugh with the rest, and when the talk was about women I had to invent conquests of my own. I hated myself at such moments, but there seemed to be nothing else that I could do. My whole life became a lie.

I thought perhaps that if I tried very hard I could, even now, wipe out the past and begin again, forcing myself to be like everybody else. I fiercely wanted to fall in love, marry and have children, as all my friends did; but this was only an abstract idea which seemed to fade away whenever I tried to think of a particular woman as a lover or a wife. Like most homosexuals, I got on very well with women, particularly in the early stages of an acquaintanceship. I could talk to them and dance with them and admire them; but sooner or later they expected me to take a more serious interest in them, and at that point I became afraid. I wanted comradeship, not possession; trust, not tension; peace and quiet, not the interminable duologue of male and female. There were many women whom I liked, but I could not imagine spending the next fifty years alone with them.

I went on trying, however. This may sound cold-blooded, but at least, on these occasions, I was not being deceitful. It seemed to me dishonest to pick on some unsuspecting girl, marry her, and run the risk of her finding out, perhaps years later, that I had used her as a kind of cure. I have no doubt that many successful marriages have begun with such a deception, but I still consider it wrong. Anyone who married me, I decided, must do so with a full knowledge of the facts.

Even so, it was difficult to avoid hurting anyone. Every relationship into which I entered with a woman was, for me, in the nature of an experiment. For her, however, it was always something deeper. A woman can never quite believe in homo-sexual desires; or rather, she underestimates them in the light of her own superior attractions. She may accept the fact that a man has succumbed to such temptations in the past, but she cannot believe that he will do so in the future. When a man turns away from other men and seeks her out, she is con-vinced that the change in him is permanent. In some cases it may be, but not, I felt, in mine.

If I married, it would be necessary for me to be completely faithful to my wife. The ordinary contract of marriage would be reinforced by the secret which we shared; having been accepted for what I was, I would owe her more than any other man would owe his wife. To resume, however intermittently, my former way of life would be to abuse the trust which she had placed in me, and to jeopardize the future of our children. I remembered what had happened to the two sons of Oscar Wilde.

I knew by now that I could not prevent myself from being attracted towards other men, however hard I might try not to be. The temptation would always be present, even if I never

38

gave way to it. Homosexuality is a condition of the mind, and it would continue to colour my whole outlook, so that I could never engage in the distinctive interchange of opposing points of view which makes a successful partnership in marriage. This was cruelly summed-up by the brother-in-law of a girl to whom I was on the point of becoming engaged. When she asked him whether she ought to marry me, he replied: 'I always advise women to marry men.'

＊

These love-affairs, into which I entered with such high hopes, always ended in regrets and unhappiness. Perhaps I was too scrupulous, or too much of a coward; in each one, at some point I began to search feverishly for a way out, realizing that once again I had made a mistake from which I must extract myself with as little cruelty as possible. It says a great deal for the natural charity of women that those whom I involved in these experiments have remained my friends; they have forgiven, even if they do not understand.

I was caught up again in the current of my inclinations, of which I had never ceased to be aware. I began to lead my double life again – almost, this time, with a feeling of relief. At least I was not deceiving myself any more, even though I was once more obliged to deceive others.

The homosexual world, invisible to almost all who do not live in it, was still as extensive as it had been immediately after the war. In London, there were still a great many men, outwardly 'respectable', who were in immediate danger of imprisonment because they had chosen to live with another man. They did not seem to care. I used to see them at theatrical first-nights and in the clubs which were patronized by homosexuals, discreetly dressed, careful in their behaviour – the last people ever to be suspected by that legendary character, the man-in-the-street. The clubs where they congregated usually consisted of one room, with a bar and a piano. They were extraordinarily quiet and well-behaved. The clubs closed at 11 o'clock, and most of the men did not go there primarily to drink, but to relax in an atmosphere where it was not necessary to keep up any pretences. This did not, however, mean that anything disreputable ever took place there. The proprietors of the clubs were not taking any chances. There was always the possibility of a raid. The police did not interfere very much with the clubs, but on one occasion they did swoop on the best-known of them and, examining the membership book, remarked on the fact that most of the clientèle appeared to be male. The proprietor coldly replied: 'You might say the same of the Athenaeum. Or, for that matter, of the Police Force.'

The public-houses which had become recognized as meeting-places for homosexuals were less discreet and a good deal more dangerous. With one or two inexplicable exceptions, they were always being raided, and 'warned' by the police. The effect of these raids was that the entire clientèle would transfer its custom, by some mysterious means of mutual agreement, to another pub, which for several months would be crowded night after night, until it was raided in its turn. This assiduity on the part of the police was presumably intended to break up the homosexual coteries, but it had the opposite effect. It was about as sensible as trying to break up a snowball by pushing it downhill.

In this world I found much to deplore, but occasionally I saw something to admire. There were many men who, in spite of the legal and social handicaps of their condition, managed to lead lives which were at least as moral as those of most heterosexuals whom I knew. They remained faithful to the partner they had chosen, and although they did not go out of their way to flout convention, they were ready to defy it for the sake of someone whom they loved. When I am embittered or revolted by the conduct of someone like myself, I try to remember two men. One was a young pianist with a brilliant talent, who killed himself for grief after the death of the man he loved. The other was a surgeon, respected and discreet, who threw away his good name in order to remain, night and day, at the bedside of his friend who was dying in hospital. A love which can evoke courage and sacrifice like this cannot, I think, be wholly evil.

I acquired an extraordinarily large circle of acquaintances, but not many friends. Most of the people whom I met were connected in some way with my job. One of these was Lord

Montagu of Beaulieu. He was a few years younger than I was and we had been at Oxford at the same time, but had not known each other there. We were introduced by another member of a firm of publicity agents with whom Lord Montagu was working; his job was to get paragraphs about various products and places into the Press, and as I was writing a gossip column at the time each of us was a useful 'contact' for the other. Furthermore, I liked him. He was one of the most completely unsnobbish people I had ever met, and I thought this a remarkable quality in an Old Etonian who had been a peer from the age of three. Although he almost certainly did not subscribe to my own somewhat anarchic social views, he was equally at home amongst all kinds of people.

The worst snobs, I have found, are those men and women who are unsure of their own social position, but the disease is by no means confined to them. Broadly speaking, there are three main kinds of British snob. There is the titled or wealthy snob, who despises everyone who does not share these advantages. There is the middle-class snob who has attained a certain place on the social ladder, from which he pours scorn on the occupants of the lower rungs and criticizes those on the higher for being no better than they should be. And there is the upside-down snob or Plain Working Man who accuses everyone, indiscriminately, of putting on airs and looking down their noses at him. The last is slightly less common than the others, but even more tedious.

I do not suppose it ever occurred to Edward Montagu that there were certain dangers in rejecting the class-system which so many of his friends and neighbours held sacred. He did it quite unconsciously. His guests, both at Beaulieu and in his London flat, formed an extraordinary assortment of conflicting types: business men and writers, Duchesses and model-girls, restaurateurs and politicians and musical comedy actresses and Guards officers and Americans wearing hand-painted ties. He was always intensely busy and often merely used to introduce his guests to each other and then disappear; a most disconcerting habit. I remember him doing this once in the middle of luncheon, leaving two big businessmen and a Canadian ice-hockey player staring at each other and wondering what on earth to talk about. Trivial though it may seem, this kind of behaviour enraged some people who took themselves extremely seriously and expected Lord Montagu to do the same. He made enemies, as well as friends.

At this time I was living in a small flat in Roland Gardens, South Kensington. It consisted of a sitting-room, bed-room, and combined kitchen-bathroom. The electric stove was in the entrance hall and the same sink did duty for both ablutions and washing up. I mentioned these facts because of the tendency of the prosecution at my trial to invest my living conditions with an air of sinful luxury. As a matter of fact, they were rather primitive, considering the rent that I was paying.

I met Eddie McNally on a rainy night in Piccadilly Circus. He was carrying a cardboard suitcase and wearing civilian clothes; during all the time that I knew him, I never saw him in uniform. He was 23 years old and had a broad Scottish accent. He was a corporal in the RAF and worked in a hospital at Ely.

I have already described the beginnings of the quest which I had carried on, almost from childhood, for an ideal companion; someone strong, courageous and reliable, who could supply all the deficiencies of my own character. I had met many who appeared, for a time at least, to fit the description – but Eddie McNally was not one of them. Perhaps the most ironical aspect of all that followed lies in the fact that my downfall was caused by someone so far removed from all that I admired.

Eddie McNally was weak, he was effeminate and – worst of all – he was one of those people whom I have described as an upside-down snob. He would hold forth for hours on the shortcomings of the 'ruling classes', who apparently existed only for the purpose of coming between Eddie McNally and his rightful deserts. But everything would be all right if only he could get some education. Education was a kind of fairy gold which lucky rich people like me received, whether they deserved it or not, while it was for ever denied to people like himself. Every discussion ended with the monotonous refrain: 'Of course, I've got no education.'

He annoyed me intensely, but at the same time I felt sorry

for him. I knew, after all, plenty of people who had received Education without being sufficiently intelligent to benefit from it, and it might be perfectly true that he would have deserved it more than they. However, it was not my mission in life to go around educating people whom I did not particularly like. The whole point about Pygmalion was that he was in love with his dumb statue.

I discovered later, however, that Eddie was one of those people whom it was impossible to get rid of. Worse still, he 'grew on' one, like ivy. He invited himself round to my flat on several occasions, and I found myself becoming fascinated by his hurt and angry view of the world. Why did he hate people like me so much? And, hating us, why did he seek our company? Why, indeed, was I beginning to seek his?

It is almost impossible to tell, in retrospect, the truth about any human relationship; particularly when it has resulted in as much agony and shame as that between Eddie McNally and myself. He insinuated himself into my life. We learned, first, to tolerate, and later to like one another. Finally, there grew up between us an extraordinary, passionate tension which resulted in quarrels when we were together and misery when we were apart.

The letters which were read in court, and McNally's evidence in the witness box, did not tell the whole story. They were given a subtly false twist which suggested that he, a simple young airman, had been dazzled by the 'lavish hospitality' with which I overwhelmed him. As a matter of fact he disliked anything lavish, and preferred to spend his visits to me playing gramophone records in the flat and helping me to cook meals on the stove in the hall. Occasionally we would make an expedition to the Tower of London or Kew Gardens, which was the kind of outing which he preferred to an evening at the theatre.

One day he suggested that we should spend our summer holiday together. I had already decided to have a quiet and inexpensive holiday that year, preferably near the sea, and Edward Montagu had previously offered to lend me his beach-hut near Beaulieu for as long as I liked. It was a Spartan, two-room building to which water had to be brought in milk-

43

churns, but it looked as though it might be pleasant enough in fine weather. Although I had some writing work to do, I did not particularly want to be alone all the time, and it seemed quite a good idea to take Eddie McNally along with me. He could help with the cooking and washing-up and take it in turns to fetch the milk from the farm a mile away. He agreed to come, but said he had already half-promised to spend his summer leave with an RAF friend, John Reynolds, and asked whether it would be all right to bring him, too.

It seemed only sensible that I should meet Reynolds before the holiday began, so I asked both of them to come round to the flat on their next week-end leave. In the meantime I had mentioned the plan to Edward, and as McNally was with me at the time he invited us both to have a drink with him at his flat in Mount Street. The flat was, as usual, full of people – Americans, I think – and we only stayed about half an hour, discussing arrangements for the holiday.

Later, McNally wrote to me, saying that he and Reynolds wanted to see a play called *Dial M for Murder*, at the Westminster Theatre, and asking whether I could book any seats. It was difficult to do this at such short notice, but I remembered that Edward Montagu had an account with a ticket agency, so I asked him if he could get two seats for the airmen whom I was bringing down to stay at his beach hut. As neither of us had seen the play, Edward suggested that he should book four seats and that we should all go together.

The play was about the efforts of a Wimbledon tennis-player to get rid of his wife by means of a perfect crime; I remember being particularly impressed by the performance of Mr Andrew Cruickshank as an obese but nimble detective from Scotland Yard. It was only eighteen months later, however, that I realized how minutely accurate this portrait had been.

When the play was over we went back to my flat for supper, stopping on the way at Mount Street to collect something to drink from the refrigerator in Edward Montagu's kitchen. It is typical of the false veil of sinful glamour subsequently thrown over the whole affair that the prosecution should have pretended that this was a bottle of champagne. As it happened, it was champagne cider; one bottle of cider, shared by four.

The holiday began more or less according to plan. Lord Montagu was spending that week-end at Beaulieu with a large house-party, and when McNally and I arrived by train from London he met us at the station, took us into Lymington to buy provisions, and deposited us at the beach hut. Reynolds had been delayed, but arrived later that evening and was brought down to the hut by Edward with some of his house-guests. Some sandwiches and a few bottles of wine were also brought down, by way of supper.

The party which followed has achieved more notoriety than any other since the days of Nero, but I feel bound to confess that it was, in fact, extremely dull. I was feeling rather tired, having been travelling all morning and swimming most of the afternoon. The two airmen sampled the contents of every bottle in sight and became slightly obnoxious, so that I began to wonder whether it had been a good idea to invite them after all. One of the other guests performed his party-piece, which was a rather boring imitation of a champion figure-skater; this encouraged the airmen to throw themselves about in all directions, whooping. I wished heartily that they would all go away. I apologize for this disappointing account, but I insist that there was no dancing between males and no activities which could be described as improper. As a matter of fact, throughout the evening the hut was encircled by Girl Guides, apparently engaged in bird-watching; a fact which does not suggest that anything very lascivious was taking place.

Edward was returning to London next day, so I had to face the prospect of remaining in the hut with Reynolds and McNally, with the possibility of a change in the weather and no transport in which to make my escape. There were no shops or telephone within walking distance. I was delighted, therefore, when Michael Pitt-Rivers suggested a way out of the difficulty.

Major Pitt-Rivers was a second cousin of Edward's, who had come to Beaulieu for the week-end to discuss business matters connected with his estate, a considerable farming property in Dorset which he managed himself. He was a man with a highly distinguished war record and a member of the Dorset County Council; a 'gentleman farmer', in fact. I had met him only once before, but had known his brother and sister-in-law for some years.

The Pitt-Rivers estate contained a curious group of buildings, standing on the outskirts of Cranborne Chase, which had been assembled in Victorian times by Michael's great-grandfather, a famous archaeologist. His object, I think, was to show the local rustics how people in other countries and at other times had lived: the result was that around a lawn in a forest clearing there now stood, in various stages of dilapidation, a Burmese house, a bandstand, a kind of Oriental theatre, and a small Greek temple. The public were no longer admitted to these grounds, which were known as the Larmer Tree, but there was an excellent museum not far away containing part of the Pitt-Rivers collection of antiquities, the remainder – which I had often visited – being housed at Oxford.

I had arranged to be away from London for a week, and did not want to cut short my holiday. Michael asked me to come and stay at the Larmer Tree, but I explained that I could hardly leave the two airmen stranded at the beach hut. It was therefore decided that they should come too. Michael would not be able to spend much of his time with us, but as he had a car we should not be entirely cut off, as we were at the beach hut. I should be able to explore the museum and get on with my writing; the two airmen could make themselves useful by helping to clear the grounds, which were overgrown with brambles and weeds.

It was a very happy arrangement. The weather was blazingly hot, and we spent several afternoons bathing at the coast. The Larmer Tree had a strange atmosphere of its own, compounded of Victorian earnestness, the incongruity of a film set, and the benevolent silence of an ancient forest. The museum contained many rare and beautiful things, including a pottery figure of a horse made by an ancestor of mine, Ralph Wood of Burslem, who had been a celebrated craftsman at a time when one of Michael's forebears, William Pitt, had occupied No. 10 Downing Street.

I shall always remember that week with pleasure, in spite of everything that has happened since. I was happy, and I had no feeling of foreboding; no suspicion of what was to come.

Not long after the holiday ended, however, I saw something which deeply shocked and angered me.

One night, when I had been working late at the office, I was walking along the Brompton Road towards my flat. Outside a closed public-house in a side turning I noticed two men loitering. A man aged about seventy, with white hair, walked past them and went into a lavatory at the side of the public-house. He was followed in by the younger of the two men. Almost immediately there was a sound of scuffling and shouting, and the older of the two whom I had first noticed also ran into the lavatory. He and his companion dragged the old man out, each holding him by an arm. He was struggling and crying.

My first thought was that they must be local 'roughs' who were trying to rob the old man, so I went towards them and shouted at them to let him go, or I would call the police.

The younger man said: 'We are Police Officers.'

A woman who had joined us on the street corner asked what the old man had done, and was told that he had been 'making a nuisance of himself'. He had now begun to struggle violently, and the two detectives pushed him up against the railings of the Cancer Hospital, outside which we were standing. His head became wedged between two iron spikes, and he started to scream. The detectives asked if one of us would ring up Chelsea Police Station and ask for a van to be sent: 'Just tell them we're at the top of Dovehouse Street, they'll know what it's about.'

The woman said: 'You can do your own dirty work, damn you.' It seemed to me, however, that the old man might be seriously injured if he continued to struggle, so I went into a telephone box a few yards away, telephoned the police station and spoke to the duty sergeant. He was evidently expecting a message, because the van arrived almost immediately. The old man, who by this time was lying on the pavement in a pool of blood, was picked up and taken away.

It was quite obvious what had happened. The younger and better-looking of the two policemen had been sent into the lavatory for the purpose of acting as an *agent-provocateur*. It was his duty to behave in such a way that some homosexual would make advances to him. The old man had fallen into the trap, and he would now be prosecuted and perhaps imprisoned. The young policeman, having behaved like a male prostitute, would probably be commended for his night's work. And, to-morrow night, he would be back there again.

*

During that year I did not see much of McNally: I was working hard and spent most of my time looking for a house. I was tired of living in an expensive but by no means luxurious two-room flat in the 'smart' district of South Kensington, and decided to move to some other part of London with lower rents and less pretensions to gentility.

After looking at various houses in Hackney and Bow, I was recommended by a friend to go to Islington, where a number of war-damaged Regency and Georgian houses were being repaired, redecorated, and let on long leases. I discovered that Canonbury, the part of Islington in which these houses stood, was an attractive place standing on high ground to the North of the City of London, the existence of which I had not suspected. The house which I inspected had been uninhabited for some time and was full of dust and rubble, but it was obvious that it could be made extremely pleasant. There was a small garden containing a pear-tree as tall as the house, a fanlight over the front door and balconies outside the first-floor windows. I signed the lease, chose the wall-paper and started to buy carpets and furniture.

In August, 1953 – a month before I was due to move in – Edward Montagu told me of a strange incident which had occurred at Beaulieu during the Bank Holiday period. Palace House, as usual, had been open to the public, and a troop of local Boy Scouts had acted as guides for the visitors. Edward and one of his guests, a film director named Kenneth Hume, had gone down to the beach hut with two of the Scouts to bathe; later Edward discovered that an expensive camera was missing, and informed the police. The latter, however, when they came to interview him about the loss, appeared to be less interested in the camera than in Lord Montagu and Mr Hume. The boys, apparently, had complained that an indecent attack had been made upon them in the beach hut.

I thought at the time – and I still think – that this was an extremely unlikely story. If Edward had had anything to hide, the last thing he would have done would be to telephone the local police station and ask for an inquiry. But I could see that the matter, if pressed any further, could result in a great deal of publicity. What made the whole business doubly unfortunate (and, in my view, even less credible) was that only a week or two before this he had announced his engagement to Miss Anne Gage, an intelligent and pretty girl with whom he was obviously very much in love.

I was now in a peculiarly awkward situation. The Press had not yet got wind of the police inquiries, so I had to be extremely careful in what I said to my colleagues in Fleet Street. Unfortunately another journalist – ironically enough, himself a homosexual – heard the story and conceived it to be his duty to tell everyone within earshot. The result was a series of little paragraphs in the newspapers, plaintively inquiring: Where is Lord Montagu?

By this time, Edward had gone abroad, hoping to avoid the rising tide of gossip and innuendo. His sister was shortly to be married and he intended to stay out of England until after the wedding. His plans, however, were cut short by the issue of a warrant for his arrest.

I shall not write about this case in any detail, except in so far as it affected my own trial. Although I did not believe that the charges against Edward Montagu were true, I shared the general public view that the crime of which he was accused was a serious one, which called for investigation and, if proved, punishment. At the same time, it hurt me deeply to know that someone whom I liked so much should be placed in such an agonizing situation. It was intolerable for me to have to listen to the sniggering little jokes about him which were current at that time, told, often enough, by men whose own sexual credentials were not above suspicion. It seemed sometimes as though every pansy in London was telling 'Montagu stories' in a feverish attempt to divert suspicion from himself.

I was, perhaps, too outspoken in my championship of Edward at this time; but, of course, I had no idea that the net which had been cast for him was soon to be expanded to include myself. In spite of certain indications to the contrary, I still believed, with many others, that the police were only interested in invoking the existing sex laws against people who had corrupted children or committed a public nuisance. A man whom I knew had, in fact, been reassured on this point by a senior official at Scotland Yard, who told him that if he was ever blackmailed he would be quite safe in going to the police, who were more concerned with catching blackmailers than with persecuting their victims.

I had forgotten, however, that there was now a new Commissioner of Police at Scotland Yard. On October 25th, 1953, while Edward was awaiting trial, the *Sydney Morning Telegraph* published a cable from its London correspondent, Mr Donald Horne, about a 'Scotland Yard plan to smash homosexuality in London'. Since the British Press, at this time, reported merely that Sir David Maxwell Fyfe, the Home Secretary, was calling for 'a new drive against male vice', it may be worth quoting the rather fuller picture presented to Australian readers.

'The plan originated,' wrote Mr Horne, 'under strong United States advice to Britain to weed out homosexuals – as hopeless security risks – from important Government jobs.

'One of the Yard's top-rankers, Commander E. A. Cole, recently spent three months in America consulting with FBI officials in putting finishing touches to the plan. But the plan was extended as a war on all vice when Sir John Nott-Bower took over as the new Commissioner at Scotland Yard in August. Sir John swore he would rip the cover off all London's filth spots. . . .

'Under laxer police methods before the US-inspired plan began, and before Sir John moved into the top job at the Yard as a man with a mission, Montagu and his film-director friend Kenneth Hume might never have been charged with grave offences against Boy Scouts. . . .

'Sir John swung into action on a nation-wide scale. He enlisted the support of local police throughout England to step up the number of arrests for homosexual offences.

'For many years past the police had turned a blind eye to male vice. They made arrests only when definite complaints were made from innocent people, or where homosexuality had encouraged other crimes.

'They knew the names of thousands of perverts – many of high social position and some world famous—but they took no action. Now, meeting Sir John's demands, they are making it a priority job to increase the number of arrests. . . .

'The Special Branch began compiling a "Black Book" of known perverts in influential Government jobs after the disappearance of the diplomats Donald Maclean and Guy Burgess, who were known to have pervert associates. Now comes the difficult task of side-tracking these men into less important jobs – or of putting them behind bars.'

As I was by now Diplomatic Correspondent of the *Daily Mail*, and visited the Foreign Office every day, I had, of course, heard of the persecution of homosexuals in the United States, where hundreds of men were being sacked from the State Department, on suspicion alone, with a ferocity only equalled by the McCarthy campaign against alleged Communist sympathizers. The excuse was that such men, having something to conceal, were more likely than others to be blackmailed into carrying out spying activities for foreign powers. The witch-hunt against homosexuals had drawn many protests, both in America and in Britain, and it seemed inconceivable that it should be extended to this country.

Much later, I happened to see an issue of *Collier's Magazine* which described the state of affairs in America at the time when Commander Cole was over there, picking up hints. The entire Vice Squads of two US cities had just been sent to prison for living on immoral earnings of prostitutes. There had been numerous cases of homosexual suspects being forced to pay 'hush-money' to the police. In some States, young children of both sexes were being trained to go out on to the streets, so that they might trap a potential sex-criminal. The conclusion drawn by the writer was that the current US sex laws were such as positively to encourage wrong-doing, particularly on the part of the police, and that they should therefore be changed. The conclusion drawn by Scotland Yard appears to have been rather different.

During the early part of December I was in Paris, attending the annual conference of the NATO Council. It was there, in the office of the *Daily Mail*, that I heard the result of the Montagu trial. The jury had acquitted Edward on the more serious charge, but had failed to agree on a lesser charge which the Director of Public Prosecutions had chosen to bring in at the last moment, without informing Edward, his counsel or solicitors. There would therefore be a re-trial on this count alone, presumably after a delay of several more months.

This seemed to me a cruel and ludicrous result. The acquittal on the graver charge showed that the jury had decided that the boy scout was lying, and the logical course would therefore have been to reject his evidence altogether. The justice of these re-trials, which have become such a feature of English judicial procedure, seems to me in any case to be open to doubt. In any trial, the onus of proof is on the prosecution; if, therefore, the prosecution fails to convince a majority of the jury that its version of the facts is correct, the benefit of the doubt should surely be given to the accused man. It seems grossly unfair that jury after jury should be empanelled until a set of twelve men is at last found who are prepared to believe the accusations brought by the Crown. This is particularly true in a case like Edward's, in which the enormous amount of publicity makes it impossible for any jury to listen to the evidence with an open mind.

In spite of this, I believed that Edward would be acquitted. After the first trial had ended, some new evidence came to light which would, I think, have exposed the whole series of accusations against him as a lie.

*

There was one feature of this case which did not, perhaps, attract as much attention from the Press as it deserved. This was the matter of Edward's passport, which he had surrendered to the police on his return to England to stand trial, and which had been in their possession ever since.

In the witness-box, Edward said that he had flown to France on August 24th, and from there to New York on September 25th. He had returned to London by air on November 7th. When he was cross-examined by Mr Fox-Andrews, QC, the counsel for the prosecution, it was put to him that he had in fact secretly returned to this country during September and had failed to give himself up to the police.

'You say that you left Paris for the United States on September 25th?' asked Mr Fox-Andrews.

Edward replied that he had.

'Did you ever go back to England between the time you went to Paris on the 24th of August and the date you left for New York on the 25th of September?'

'I did not.'

'You did not?'

'No.'

'Look at page seven of your passport. . . . Can you explain that entry in that passport which indicates that you left Boulogne on the 23rd of September?'

'Only the French Customs could explain that.'

'You see the entry, don't you, and the date?'

'Yes.'

'That indicates an exit from Boulogne on the 23rd September, does it not?'

'All I can say is that I was in Paris at that time, that I went direct to America from Paris, and that I have not been in Boulogne since 1948,' said Edward.

'And you can give no explanation of that entry about Boulogne in your passport?'

'None whatever.'

'May I,' asked Mr Fox-Andrews, 'make a suggestion? Is it possible that you may have forgotten, and that you may have flown to England – and that you may have flown to America from England on the 25th of September?'

'I did not; I flew from France.'

Mr Fox-Andrews continued to suggest that Edward was not telling the truth; Edward continued to insist that he had been nowhere near Boulogne on the date shown on the passport. The Judge, looking at the passport, asked him: 'When did you go to Boulogne?' Edward replied that it was in 1948 or 1949.

After carefully examining the entry, the Judge, Mr Justice Lynskey, remarked: 'This entry in this passport has obviously been altered, Mr Fox-Andrews.'

The judge then directed that the passport should be shown to the jury, while the matter was fresh in their minds. 'You will

53

see "Boulogne", members of the jury,' he said, 'in the left-hand corner. You may think that the "5" looks as if it had been "4". You will each form your own view about that.' He turned to Edward and said: 'That passport has not been in your hands since it was taken from you on your arrival in this country?'

'That is so, my Lord. I can prove exactly what I did on the 23rd of September.'

I have quoted this dialogue at some length, because it seems to me to disclose a very singular state of affairs. An important piece of Crown evidence had been exposed as a forgery. The passport had been altered, quite obviously, in order to prove that Edward Montagu was a liar. If the jury could be convinced that he was lying about his movements, they might naturally conclude that his other evidence could not be believed. The forged passport was thus a powerful weapon in the hands of the Crown.

The matter of the passport was brought up again during the second case, in which I was involved myself. No attempt was ever made by the prosecution to explain it. It was apparently accepted as normal that the police should produce forged documents as evidence, in the same way that it was accepted that they should search a house without a warrant, re-arrest a man while he was on bail on another charge, terrorize McNally and Reynolds by repeated questionings and promise them immunity from prosecution if they would give evidence against their former friends.

I did not believe that such things could happen in England, until they happened to me.

PART TWO

BETWEEN Edward's arrest and the opening of his trial I wrote to him, wishing him luck – a letter which was subsequently produced by the prosecution during my own trial. I had not seen McNally for some time, but one evening in a public-house in Bloomsbury I happened to meet Reynolds. He left the group with whom he had been drinking and came over to speak to me. He was very agitated about the arrest and said that when he and McNally had read the news they had been very upset, fearing that I was 'the friend of Lord Montagu' who had been charged at the same time. I told him that I was in no way implicated in the case.

At the end of November McNally came to see me at Canonbury, bringing two long-playing gramophone records as a present. I think we both realized that we should not be seeing each other any more; we had quarrelled several times and I had been somewhat disturbed to hear from him that his family had been going through his pockets and had discovered one of my letters. He told me that he was due to leave the RAF in a few months' time and suggested that I might employ him as a man-servant. I turned down this idea, partly because I already had a man-servant and partly because there was something about McNally's appearance and behaviour which made me uneasy. He repeated the story about the letter, saying that his father still had it. Previously, he had assured me that it had been destroyed. I decided that the wisest course would be to see no more of him.

I returned to London and resumed my work. The Editor told me that now, after a six-month trial period, my appointment as Diplomatic Correspondent was definitely confirmed. I celebrated this event by inviting my mother and father to spend Christmas with me in my new house. I put up a Christmas tree and paper chains, and a holly-wreath in the window, immensely proud to be entertaining my parents in a house which I had bought and furnished entirely out of my own earnings. That Christmas, I was completely happy.

I was due to go to Berlin for the four-Power conference of Foreign Ministers on January the 14th. On Friday, January the 8th, I visited the Foreign Office as usual, went to the *Daily Mail* office and returned to my home at about 11 p.m. My man-servant, whose room was in the basement, had been ill for a few days and the doctor had been to see him. I said good-night to him and went upstairs to bed.

At 8 o'clock the next morning there was a thunderous knocking at the door. I ran downstairs in pyjamas and dressing-gown and opened it. Three men were standing outside, wearing mackintoshes and trilby hats. One of them said: 'Are you Mr Wildeblood?' I told him that I was. He said: 'We are police officers from the Hampshire Constabulary and from New Scotland Yard. We have come to arrest you, Wildeblood, for offences arising out of your association with Edward McNally and John Reynolds in the summer of 1952.'

It was a bitterly cold morning, and when I heard these words, so incongruous in their stilted language, I felt as though I was drowning in an icy sea. I could not speak. I was shaking violently as they pushed past me into the hall. The one who had spoken before asked: 'Where do you sleep?' I told him that my bedroom was on the second floor.

'Anybody up there with you?'

'No, of course not.'

'Anyone else in the house?'

I told him that the man-servant, who had been ill for several days, was in the basement, asleep. One of the detectives detached himself from the group and went downstairs. The other two, it appeared, were Detective Superintendent Jones, of the Hampshire Police, and Detective Superintendent Smith, of Scotland Yard's Special Branch. I had already heard of Superintendent Jones. He had been in charge of the first Montagu Case.

'We are going to search the house,' said Superintendent Jones. He did not, however, produce a warrant. I tried to remember – were the police allowed to search a house without a warrant? My numb and frozen mind refused to give me an answer.

'I must get in touch with my solicitor,' I said.

'That can wait. We've got plenty of time.'

Then they began to ask questions. Had I spent a holiday at Beaulieu and in Dorset in 1952? Had I been to see *Dial M for Murder*? Did I have the programme? Or the ticket stubs? Or the envelope in which they had been sent from the ticket agency?

I said, again, that I wanted to telephone my solicitor.

'He won't be at his office yet,' said Superintendent Jones. He was a big swarthy Welshman, running to fat but with the remains of a flashy handsomeness.

'He doesn't go to his office on Saturday mornings,' I said. 'But there's a Christmas card from him in my desk, with his home number on it.'

'Well, you can't touch anything on the desk until we've finished going through it. Have you any photographs of McNally?'

I took some from a drawer. They were mixed up with other photographs of my mother and father, and of their cottage in Sussex.

With a flourish, Superintendent Jones produced a bundle of letters from his briefcase. 'Is this your handwriting?' he asked.

I looked at the top letter. It was one which I had written to McNally; a poor, trusting, foolish letter born of loneliness and a craving for affection. It lay between the detective's plump hands lightly, like a grenade.

'Yes, I wrote them,' I said.

There was a long silence, while the two men, still wearing their mackintoshes, bustled about the house, opening cupboards and chests of drawers, methodically sifting everything I possessed, going through the pockets of my suits and looking under the mattress and reading every letter that they found.

'Who's this from?'

'My mother.'

'And this? Someone in the Navy, isn't it?'

'Yes.'

He put it in his pocket. 'You're in a pretty bad position, you know,' said Superintendent Jones. 'It's a pity you ever got mixed up with that crowd. Look here, don't you think you would feel better if you made a clean breast of it?'

'I think I ought to see my solicitor first.'

'Well, it's up to you to decide, not him.'

Eventually – after they had spent an hour and a half searching the house – I was allowed to telephone my solicitor. He said that he did not feel qualified to deal with the matter, but that he would ring up his father (the senior partner in his firm) and ask him to recommend someone.

The questions went on.

Although I did not yet know the gravity of the charges against me, I realized that the whole of my relationship with McNally was going to be dragged out into the light. My letters to him would be read in public. I could imagine the effect on my parents. I should lose everything for which I had worked: my job, my home, my friends. I thought of killing myself.

'May I go up to the bathroom?'

Superintendent Smith, an avuncular man with smooth grey hair, said: 'All right, but don't go doing anything silly.' He made me leave the bathroom door ajar, and stood outside while I shaved. In the cold, flat light of a January morning, my reflection in the mirror looked fantastically like a criminal's identity photograph.

When I went downstairs again, I said: 'What is going to happen to me?'

Superintendent Jones fixed his very pale blue eyes upon me and said: 'Well, I make it a rule never to make promises; but as you haven't been in trouble before I should think you'd probably get bound over. The best thing is for you to make a statement. You just clear yourself – don't bother too much about the others.'

The telephone rang. It was my solicitor. He said that Mr Harry Myers, who specialized in criminal cases, had agreed to take over. I asked him to tell Mr Myers to come to the house as soon as he could. I told him not to worry too much, as I understood that I should probably get bound over. At this point Superintendent Smith tapped me on the arm and said: 'Don't discuss the case over the telephone. Tell him to get Myers to ring me at the Yard – we'll be going there presently.'

I afterwards discovered that during the three and a half hours which the two Superintendents spent in searching the house, the Sergeant who accompanied them had been questioning my man-servant. This man was in no possible way connected with the case, not having been in my employment in 1952; but he was made to get out of bed, his room searched and his correspondence read.

While Superintendent Jones was going through the contents of my wallet he found a number of visiting cards and telephone numbers, mainly belonging to business 'contacts'. Noticing one well-known name among them, he asked: 'I suppose he's queer too?' I said that if they really wanted a list of homosexuals from me I would be happy to oblige, beginning with judges, policemen, and members of the Government. I was beginning to feel slightly better. Very faintly, as though at the end of a tunnel, I could see what I must do. I would make a statement, but it would not be of the kind which Superintendent Jones was expecting. Far from incriminating Edward Montagu and Michael Pitt-Rivers, as he hoped, I would simply tell the truth about myself. I had no illusions about the amount of publicity which would be involved. I would be the first homosexual to tell what it felt like to be an exile in one's own country. I might destroy myself, but perhaps I could help others.

At Scotland Yard, I was allowed to telephone to a friend and ask him to be at Lymington Police Station at 5.30 p.m., when I was to be charged, so that he could stand bail for me. At the same time, Superintendent Smith was apparently speaking to Mr Myers on another extension; he came into the room where I was sitting and said: 'Mr Myers won't be here for some time yet. Would you like to start writing your statement now?' I said that I would, and Superintendent Jones produced from his briefcase a sheaf of Hampshire Constabulary statement forms which he had evidently brought with him for the purpose.

It is, I think, significant that Jones, the senior police officer in charge of the whole operation, should have come to arrest me, while the arrests of Montagu and Pitt-Rivers were carried out by subordinates. Possibly he hoped that I could be induced to make an incriminating statement which would implicate the others. I did not realize at this time, of course, that I was to be charged with conspiring with the other two to incite Reynolds and McNally to commit indecent acts. This was a clever legal move on the part of the Director of Public Prosecutions, so that my letters – regarded as strong corroborative evidence – could be used not only against me, but against Lord Montagu, who was of course the real quarry.

*

The statement which I made was never read out in court, because my counsel successfully pleaded that it was not a voluntary statement and was therefore inadmissible as evidence. I should perhaps explain that it was in no sense a 'confession', although I admitted, as I did later in court, that I was a homosexual, and attempted to give some account of the difficulties inherent in my condition.

After I had made this statement I was allowed to see Mr Myers. It was now five hours since I had first asked to get in touch with my solicitor. During the trial the police, when cross-examined about this delay, said that it had been made necessary by the large scale and complexity of the police operations that morning. Since all three of us had been arrested by 8.15 a.m. this was obviously untrue, but it was apparently accepted by the judge. Both Edward and Michael were prevented in the same way from seeing their solicitors. The police, in fact, were giving the news of our arrest to the Press several hours before we were allowed to seek the legal advice which was our right.

Before leaving Scotland Yard I telephoned the News Editor of the *Daily Mail*, Mr Hardcastle, at his home. He had already heard the news of my arrest from a news agency message. This was three hours before I was charged. The evening papers were able to print eyewitness accounts of Lord Montagu's arrest, apparently provided by the police, before he had been allowed to see a solicitor and before he had been charged.

I was taken by car to Winchester, where I was photographed and fingerprinted at the police station. Then we went on to Lymington, where Edward and Michael were already waiting. The place was besieged by reporters and photographers. We were brought up before the magistrate, charged and formally remanded. The charges, on this first hearing, were concerned only with things we were supposed to have done in Hampshire. The police had plenty of other charges up their sleeve, concerning incidents in London and Dorset, yet they were arranging for the second trial of Lord Montagu to take place in Hampshire, where local prejudice against him might be expected to be strongest. The Hampshire charge which they brought against me on this occasion was, in fact, subsequently dropped.

That evening, I telephoned my mother and told her the news which was to be headlined in every newspaper next morning. She said: 'Whatever happens, we will stand by you.'

Next morning, I felt like a hunted fox. I had been warned that my telephone would be 'tapped', in spite of the fact that this is illegal in England. To speak to my friends I had to go out to a telephone box, passing on the way the news-stands from which my name stared out in heavy black type. I felt that it did not much matter what the verdict might be; it was a trial by smear, not a trial by jury, which I was about to undergo. But I was determined to fight the case to the last ditch.

To do this, I needed money. My bank manager, rather callously, took the opportunity of writing to tell me that I had 7s. 5d. in my account. The *Daily Mail*, however, gave me to understand that they would assist me with the legal costs, and use their influence to brief a good counsel. I was invited to visit the Legal Adviser at Carmelite House to discuss the arrangements. It was not easy to go back to Fleet Street, under the curious stares of hall porters and lift boys, but I was desperate. The Legal Adviser, an urbane and kindly person, installed me in a large leather armchair and offered me a cigarette.

It was all most unfortunate, he explained, but somebody had changed his mind. It would cause a dangerous precedent if I was assisted with my costs; other reporters charged with motoring offences might also ask for help. So he was afraid, old boy, that there was nothing he could do. Anyhow I was not to worry too much because (merciful heavens!) there probably wouldn't be that much publicity, after all. . . .

My parents drew out all their savings and several other people gave me as much as they could afford, but there still did not seem to be enough to brief a first-class counsel. I could not hope for a QC, but it was possible that some young barrister with a name to make would take the brief for a reasonable fee. The man I wanted, I decided, was Peter Rawlinson, who had defended the 'Towpath murderer', Alfred Whiteway, a few months before. In this case he had attacked the police mercilessly – a thing which, I suspected, was 'not done' in legal circles. In the meantime, however, it was agreed that Mr Myers should represent me at the magistrates' court hearing.

This began at Lymington on a very cold Saturday morning. The magistrates were mostly local shop-keepers, who seemed to be basking in the limelight which the case had attracted to their Bench; indeed, one of the court officials was so impressed that he handed round one of his documents for us all to sign, as though it were a menu card.

Before the hearing began, the three accused were faced in the hallway by Superintendent Jones, who read out to us nineteen further charges. We were now charged not only with committing certain acts, but on each occasion with conspiring together to commit them. We were, of course, reserving our defence for the higher court. The whole of the prosecution case would therefore be reported in detail in the Hampshire papers, where it would be read by anyone who was likely to be picked as a juror at the subsequent trial.

The magistrates looked somewhat shocked when Mr Fearnley-Whittingstall, representing Lord Montagu, suggested that they should exercise their right to hold the hearing *in camera*. It took them about three minutes to decide that the interests of justice would be best served by spreading the Crown allegations – many of which were subsequently disproved – all over the front pages of next morning's papers.

Mr 'Khaki' Roberts, the prosecution counsel, rose magnificently to this opportunity. He was an impressive person, with purple jowls hanging down over his collar. Occasionally, as though to underline a point, he paused in his oration and helped himself to a teaspoonful of bright pink cough-mixture from a bottle lying among his documents. His voice was fruity and passionate; it shook with horror as he described the scandalous liaison between the witnesses and the accused. It was hard to believe that only a few weeks before he had been equally sincere in the defence of Mr Rupert Croft-Cooke, the novelist, on a similar charge. In his book *The Verdict of You All* (Secker and Warburg, 1955) Mr Croft-Cooke described Mr Roberts' peroration as 'a very powerful speech, charged with sincere indignation at what I had undergone already at the hands of the police and at the prosecution's methods in general. . . . He spoke, I thought, so brilliantly, he thundered in such righteous ire . . . wholly in earnest . . . a passionate honest speech. . . .'

This time, Mr Roberts was on the other side of the fence. He introduced his two 'star' witnesses, Reynolds and McNally, with some distaste as 'men of the lowest possible moral character', who had been corrupted long before they had met us. He then alleged that the airmen had committed immoral acts 'under the seductive influence of the lavish hospitality' with which they had been loaded by Edward, Michael, and myself. This set the Press benches scribbling busily.

I thought wryly of McNally and myself cooking scrambled eggs on the stove in the hall, and going out occasionally for a pint of bitter in a pub; of the carpetless rooms in the beach hut with their shabby furniture; of the bottle of cider, shared by four.

Mr Roberts, however, was getting into his stride by now. The cider had been transmuted, as though by a miracle, into champagne. The beach hut had become a gilded den of vice in which all-male orgies went on till dawn. I became so fascinated that it was only with difficulty that I remembered that Mr Roberts was talking about me. At one moment, in order to mop his brow, he pulled a handkerchief from his coat pocket, dislodging a spare set of false teeth which shot across the floor and landed, grinning, between my feet.

Farce changed abruptly into horror when McNally entered the box. He looked pale and sulky, wearing a blue serge blazer and flannel trousers. His mouth began to open and shut like that of a ventriloquist's dummy, and what came out, I swear, was not his own voice but the voice of a policeman, drearily repeating in the official formulae the fantasies which formed the basis of the prosecution case. What was so surprising was not that his evidence was so inaccurate, but that a large proportion of the inaccuracies seemed so trivial. But all of them, however small and irrelevant, tended to corroborate the charge on which the Crown was relying to convict Lord Montagu – the charge of conspiracy.

The transformation of McNally was complete, horrible, and pathetic. It had been brought about, apparently, in the following way. The technique used should be of interest to all students of police methods.

On December 16th – the day, significantly enough, of the ending of Edward Montagu's first trial – McNally had been interviewed by a member of the RAF Special Investigation Branch about letters which had been found in his kit. These had been written by a number of men, including myself. He was again 'grilled' on December 23rd, and on the following day was arrested and charged by the RAF with indecency with male persons, no names being mentioned. He spent Christmas under close arrest, and was brought up before his CO on December 27th. In spite of his plea of Guilty, no evidence was offered and he was released 'without prejudice'. The Crown was after bigger fish than Corporal McNally.

By this time he had confessed to offences with numerous men, but the police were interested in only one name – mine. This was because, in one of my letters, I had mentioned the magic word 'Beaulieu'. Although it was pretended by the Crown that the inquiries had begun as part of a general inquiry into homosexuality in the RAF, none of the other men accused by McNally and Reynolds – of whom there were 24 – was ever prosecuted.

On December 28th Superintendent Jones arrived upon the scene, and took over the questioning of McNally from the RAF Police. Altogether McNally was interrogated for a total of 18 hours. He was first persuaded to confess by being told that Reynolds had already 'squealed'; then the threat of a prosecution was held over him, and backed up by the extra-ordinary mock trial held on December 27th; finally he was told that he would never be prosecuted for any of the offences which he had revealed, provided that he turned Queen's Evidence against Edward, Michael Pitt-Rivers, and myself.

It is, I think, rather too easy to despise the stool-pigeon in a case like this. McNally and Reynolds were, by their own admission, browbeaten into a state of such terror that they were prepared to say 'yes' (I quote Reynolds) to any question that was put to them. My own contempt is reserved for the men who permitted such a course to be taken in the name of justice. The words 'immoral' and 'obscene' have been freely used to describe the lives of men like myself. I ask: could any-thing be more immoral than the way in which the confessions of Reynolds and McNally were extorted? Could anything be more obscene than the sight of these men, under the promise of a free pardon, being dragged to court to betray those whom they had once called their friends?

I know how difficult it is for a law-abiding citizen to believe that the police, in England, acquire their evidence in such a manner; two years ago, I should have found it hard to believe, myself. We have all been brought up to believe that crime-detection is carried out by painstaking research and brilliant intuition, à la Agatha Christie; the truth is that it relies almost entirely, if this case is typical, on trapping the accused man into making an incriminating statement, or by coercing some-one else – often an accomplice – into giving evidence against him.

The deterioration in police ethics may have resulted from the post-war crime wave; it has now reached a stage where some hundreds of police officers are themselves convicted each year, usually of breaking and entering, and sometimes of blackmail. I am the first to agree that crime waves must be curbed, but not at this price.

The present trend was, incidentally, foretold with precision by H. G. Wells in *The Shape of Things to Come*. Nearly fifty years ago he wrote, in his imaginary history of the 20th Cen-tury, that the police forces, 'in spite of a notable amount of corruption and actual descents into criminality' did manage to keep up their traditional war against crime.

But their methods underwent a considerable degeneration, which was shared, and shared for the same reason, by the criminal law of the period. Police and prosecutor both felt that the dice were loaded against them, that they were battling against unfair odds. Their war against crime became a feud. It grew less and less like a serene control, and more and more like a gang conflict. They were working in an atmosphere in which witnesses were easily intimidated and local sympathy more often than not against the law. This led to an increasing unscrupulousness on their part in the tendering and treatment of evidence. In many cases (see Aubrey Wilkinson's *The Natural History of the Police Frame-up*, 1991) the police deliberately manufactured evidence against criminals they had good reason to believe guilty, and perjured themselves unhesitatingly.

While I have been writing this, two London policemen have been sent to prison for blackmailing a man by threatening to accuse him of importuning them in Piccadilly. On two consecutive days recently there have been reports of the suspension of senior police officers for undisclosed reasons, after complaints from members of the public. A lawyer, writing to the *Evening Standard*, expressed the growing public disquiet at the methods of the police.

All those who have had any great experience of criminal litigation know that evidence is frequently tendered by the police which is later shown to be false.

In all my cases of recent years when police evidence has played a material part, I have always made a practice of warning defendants under no circumstances to challenge such evidence, even though it is known to be false. Experience has proved to me that there is no surer way for a defendant to lose his case than to say in effect: the police are lying.

It would be tedious to describe in any detail the various stages in the hearing at the magistrates' court. Inevitably, we were committed for trial. The preliminary hearing had received the fullest possible publicity. From now on, Edward Montagu's name would be indelibly connected in the public mind – and therefore in the minds of the twelve men who would later try him – not only with Boy Scouts, but with all-male parties and champagne orgies. He had about as much chance of a fair trial as a Negro in the Southern States of America.

*

The weather continued to be bitterly cold. In my house, which had been so gay and cheerful at Christmas time, the life seemed to be ebbing gently away. The pipes froze. The coal supply ran out, but there seemed no point in ordering any more. There were several mysterious, anonymous telephone calls in the middle of the night; when I lifted the receiver I took to saying: 'Beware, whoever you are. This telephone has three extensions; one in the drawing-room, one in the bed-room, and one at Scotland Yard.' It was perfectly true that the line was being tapped. When I made a call, I could faintly hear someone moving about on a creaky chair, and sometimes humming, as of a recording-machine.

I still seemed to be no nearer to getting a counsel, so eventually I changed my solicitor. The new one was Arthur Prothero, a breezy ex-Naval type with a black beard who had worked with Peter Rawlinson on the 'Towpath murder' case. He succeeded in persuading Rawlinson to accept the brief, in spite of the fact that funds were still painfully low, and together we began to plan our defence.

I was determined to admit that I was a homosexual. This was not bravado; it was deliberate planning for the future. There were several signs that a full-scale inquiry into the problems of homosexuality would one day take place, and I meant to play a part in it. This I could not have done if I had taken the obvious line of defence and denied everything. I had been much encouraged in this course by hearing that Sir Robert Boothby, MP, had on several occasions pressed the Home Secretary to set up a Royal Commission to inquire into the efficacy and justice of the present laws. His campaign had gained strength recently from an unsuspected quarter – the Church of England.

The Problem of Homosexuality : an Interim Report was the title of a pamphlet issued by the Church of England Moral

67

Welfare Council shortly after I was arrested. It said that a group of Churchmen had been studying this problem for over a year, and that their full report would be published in due course; but in the meantime they had produced this preliminary draft 'in view of the concern of the public with the subject which arose after certain well-known people had been prosecuted for homosexual offences, and of the possibility that some official inquiry into the whole matter might be set on foot'. There was a real danger, the authors added, that public opinion might be inflamed by the sensational Press 'to the point of demanding persecution in addition to prosecution'.

The view of the Church was that although homosexual behaviour between consenting adults amounted to a sin, it was no worse – indeed, perhaps less harmful in its social effects – than adultery or fornication. There were certainly no grounds for treating it as a crime. The law as it stood did not merely fail to act as a deterrent; it encouraged blackmail, suicide, and the corruption of the police. In the name of justice and humanity the Church called for a change in the law, and insisted that there should be an immediate official inquiry.

This pamphlet must have come as a considerable shock to those State officials who were now in full cry after Edward Montagu, cutting, as it did, the moral ground from under their feet. It surprised me, too. I had always thought of the Church as the last stronghold of prejudice and had never found an occasion for praising it for its courage in controversial matters; yet here, from Church House, came an attack on the law which was as broad-minded, clear-headed, and brilliantly argued as one could wish. It was all the more surprising because the English laws against homosexuality were religious in origin and widely held to represent the views of the Church.

For the moment, however, our concern was with the law as it stood. Peter Rawlinson took the view that my statement to the police, however sincere, might have a damaging effect in the poisoned atmosphere of the court; he proposed to object to it on the grounds that it had been extracted – which was perfectly true – on the promises of Superintendent Jones that I would receive preferential treatment if I 'made a clean breast' of it all.

The weeks dragged on. Mr Schofield, the Editor of the *Daily Mail*, was persuaded – with some reluctance on his part – to go to Winchester Assizes as a 'character witness'. The men who had been present at the famous beach-hut party had all disappeared, and I could hardly blame them. The occasion had been represented in such lurid terms that it was as much as anyone's reputation was worth to admit having been there. It had been such a dull party, too; to be bored to death was bad enough, but to have been subsequently accused of taking part in an orgy would have been intolerable. Very prudently, they all discovered reasons for having to go abroad.

I cheered myself up by thinking of the taxi driver who had taken me from Southampton each day to the magistrates' court at Lymington. Undaunted by exploding flashbulbs and curious faces peering through the window, he had remarked: 'Personally, and speaking man to man, I think it's a lot of bleeding nonsense. If two chaps carry on like that and don't do no harm to no-one, what business is it of anybody else's?'

The trial began on March 15th, 1954, in the hall of Winchester Castle. Most of the courtrooms which I had seen during my work as a reporter were dark, solemn places, smelling of dust and leather. This was different. Its soaring stone arches had been freshly cleaned and the woodwork painted a glossy pale grey; the dock was so brightly illuminated that it appeared to be floodlit. Hanging high above the judge's throne was the top of a huge round table, supposed to be the original one used by King Arthur and his knights. It was divided into coloured sections like a Wheel of Fortune.

I sat in the dock with Edward Montagu and Michael Pitt-Rivers. Behind us there was a warder from Winchester Prison, an affable person who filled in the time by doodling endless pictures of donkeys on a sketch-pad. In front of us, at a lower level, sat the leading Counsel with their Juniors and the various solicitors – a prospect of grey and white curly wigs looking, from the dock, like a bed of cauliflowers amongst which someone had flung several cartloads of papers tied up with pink tape. Beyond these was the judge's dais, on which stood an elaborate throne and two smaller chairs for Chaplain and Sheriff. On our left was the witness-box and behind it six rows of benches for the public. On our right were the benches for the jury.

We had already decided to object to an all-male jury and to go on objecting until some women were called. We believed – and, I think, rightly – that women jurors were likely to be more fair-minded and sympathetic in a case like this. On the lengthy list of people called for jury-duty that day there was not one woman.

The twelve men who made up our jury did not look remarkable in any way. They might have been anybody, and it was strange to think that the rest of my life depended on their decision. Most of them were middle-aged, and looked like shopkeepers or farmers. There were two young men, one of whom wore a bow-tie on the first day of the trial, but afterwards exchanged it for something more severe. And there was a small, elderly person who spent most of the time curled up asleep, like the Dormouse at the Mad Hatter's tea-party.

When the nineteen charges on the indictment had been read out by the Clerk of the Court, and the three accused had pleaded Not Guilty to each one, Mr Roberts – still accompanied by his bottle of cough-mixture – launched into his opening speech. By now, I almost knew it by heart. 'Reynolds and McNally are put forward as perverts,' he thundered, 'men of the lowest possible moral character; men who were corrupted, who apparently cheerfully accepted corruption, long before they met the three defendants. It is not to be laid at the door of the defendants that they were a party to the corruption at all.

'These are witnesses whom we, in law, know as accomplices. They were willing parties to these unnatural offences, although of course, they were committed under the seductive influence of lavish hospitality from these men, who were so infinitely their social superiors. . . . '

And then he began to read the letters which, nearly two years before, had passed between McNally and me. It seemed incredible that I could have written such words to such a man; and yet, even when I heard them ringing round the court room in the voice of Mr Roberts, I recognized them as my own. I remembered the loneliness and misery of the nights when I had written them, and my desperate hope that I could find, even in McNally, someone with whom to share my life.

It was cruel enough to have to listen to them. What made it even worse was the knowledge that these letters were not only being used as evidence against myself, but against Edward and Michael, who had not even known of their existence.

McNally came into the witness-box to say his piece. Whereas, at Lymington, he had hesitated and contradicted himself on several occasions, this time he was almost word-perfect. The high, flat voice with its Scottish accent whined on, reducing everything that there had ever been between us to the text-book phrases of the police. Laughter and misery, loneliness and comradeship and love and hate, had come to this: a mean little parrot-voice that went on and on – 'Mr Wildeblood did this. Mr Wildeblood said that.'

Peter Rawlinson rose, clasped his hands behind his back, and looked at McNally as though he were something sticking to a spade. 'Would you turn your head and look at the men in the dock?' he asked. 'Is the man on the right Peter Wildeblood?'

McNally glanced at me, briefly. It was the first time he had done so. I searched his eyes with mine, looking desperately for some flicker of shame or sorrow, but there was none. His eyes were dead, like a doll's eyes.

'Yes, sir,' he said.

'During 1952 and 1953 were you what you would describe as "in love" with Peter Wildeblood?'

'Yes, sir.'

'And when you wrote him those letters of which we have heard, did you mean the expressions of sentiment which you expressed?'

'Yes, sir.'

'Let us just remind ourselves of them. In December, 1953, you said: "As for me, well, I never change." Did you mean that?'

'Yes, sir.'

'When you wrote "I'm still very much in love," did you mean that?'

'Yes, sir.'

'And the letters you wrote were quite sincere letters?'

'Yes, sir.'

'To the person whom you thought you were in love with?'

'Yes, sir.'

It was horrible. I looked round the court. The jury and the people on the public benches sat with pinched mouths and clasped hands, looking at their shoes. The judge looked as though he had bitten a lemon. The Sheriff's eyes were closed; the Chaplain's, popping. I wanted to get up and shout: 'It was not I who made "love" into a dirty word – it is you!'

Rawlinson probed and gouged McNally like a dentist drilling a rotten tooth. Out it all came: the truculence, the shamming, the squalid little affairs with half a dozen men, some of whose names he did not even know; and the more Rawlinson forced him to expose himself, the more firmly he stuck to the story which he had learned. When questioned about details he became vague and evasive, twisting, turning, contradicting his previous evidence and saying that he didn't remember; but on the main points he stood firm, repeating over and over again in the same incongruous words: 'Mr Wildeblood committed an offence against me.'

One of the facts elicited by Mr Rawlinson was that McNally, during the period when he said he was in love with me, was corresponding on even more affectionate terms with a man named Gerry. I do not know Gerry and I wish him no ill, but the fact remains that there was ten times more evidence of a sexual relationship between McNally and Gerry than there was between McNally and myself. This man's name was one of those which McNally had given to the police. We produced in court a letter in which McNally had described Gerry as 'my husband', and a receipt from the Regent Palace Hotel, where they had shared a room together. The fact that neither of them was charged with an offence proves, I think conclusively, that the Crown in this case was not even concerned with the administration of the law as it stood. It was simply out to put Lord Montagu behind bars.

It is difficult, if not impossible, to trace the origins of a witch-hunt. It may be true that the case began as a political manoeuvre, designed to allay American fears that people susceptible to blackmail were occupying high positions in Britain. The police may be criticized for their methods, but it must be remembered that the police are not all-powerful. However anxious the police chiefs in Hampshire may have been to secure a conviction against Montagu after they had lost the first case, it would have been impossible for them to proceed without encouragement from someone in a higher position.

Who was this person? The Home Secretary at this time was Sir David Maxwell Fyfe, a Scottish lawyer whose tenure of office had already been marked by the hanging of Derek Bentley, the disquiet over the Christie-Evans case, and the refusal of political asylum to Dr Cort when he was being persecuted by the American authorities. Sir David had persistently refused the requests of Sir Robert Boothby in Parliament that a Royal Commission should be set up to inquire into the nature and treatment of homosexuality. After our case ended his deputy, Sir Hugh Lucas Tooth, gave evasive and in some instances untrue replies to questions about police procedure. Later, Sir David was forced to agree to the setting-up of an official inquiry into homosexuality. A few months later, he left the Home Office, became Lord Chancellor and, by accepting a peerage, renounced the possibility of higher political office.

The Police Commissioner was Sir John Nott-Bower. It was around the time of his promotion to this post at Scotland Yard that the series of prosecutions of well-known people began. The previous policy of not interfering with people's private lives unless they were harming others was apparently reversed.

The Director of Public Prosecutions was Sir Theobald Mathew. It was on his instructions that Edward Montagu was charged with the offences (said to have happened two years before) against Reynolds, at a time when Edward was already on bail, waiting for a re-trial of the Boy Scout case. It was Sir Theobald, too, who gave the assurance that Reynolds and McNally – however many offences they might admit – would never in any circumstances be prosecuted. He took the liveliest personal interest in the case, and was present when we were sentenced.

*

73

Reynolds was, if anything, an even less impressive witness than McNally. He had already said at the magistrates' court that he had been 'terrified' by the police inquiries, and had almost wept. His evidence was so confused and contradictory that the four main charges against Montagu had to be dropped; they were simply not borne out by anything that Reynolds said in court. In cross-examination he denied that he had ever told the police that Montagu had committed these offences.

On the third day of the trial, the police gave their evidence. First, Detective Sergeant Anderson, who had searched Michael Pitt-Rivers' London flat at the time when he was being arrested in Dorset. Mr Hylton-Foster, in cross-examination, asked him: 'I appreciate, Sergeant, that you are not at the top of the Hampshire Constabulary hierarchy, and you were apparently acting on instructions; but it is a fact, is it not, that you went to this man's flat without his permission, without any sort or kind of warrant, and proceeded to search it?'

'That is so, sir,' said the Sergeant.

'I do not ask you what the law is, but are you of the opinion that the law entitled you to do that?'

Mr Roberts jumped up. 'My Lord, I object to that question. I submit that this witness' opinion of the law is entirely irrelevant. I am perfectly prepared to argue the point, and I have the authorities here.'

The judge leaned forward. 'Well, I agree,' he said, 'if it is necessary to argue it. The fact is – and it has been elicited – that he entered the premises without a warrant. We will leave it at that.'

Sergeant Toms, also of the Hampshire Police, then described how he had searched Lord Montagu's London flat, also in his absence. He, likewise, admitted in cross-examination that he had no search warrant.

Detective Inspector Stuchfield told how he had arrested Lord Montagu. He was cross-examined by Mr Fearnley-Whittingstall.

'Why was he not allowed to telephone to his solicitor?'

'In view of the magnitude of the police activities that day, and the fact that a delay of an hour would not prejudice him, I decided not to for those reasons.'

'Do you know that throughout the day he was not allowed to communicate with his solicitor?'

Mr Roberts again objected.

Later, Mr Fearnley-Whittingstall asked: 'Did his (Lord Montagu's) solicitor speak to you on the telephone?'

'Yes.'

'Did he ask you whether you had a warrant to search the house?'

'Yes.'

'Had you?'

'No.'

'You had been instructed to search, had you?'

'Yes.'

'By whom.'

'By Detective Superintendent Jones.'

Detective Inspector Stuchfield was then cross-examined about the alteration in Edward's passport.

'You will agree, will you not, that the passport had been altered in a way which, if it had not been detected as an alteration, would have conflicted with evidence that he had given on another occasion?'

'Yes.'

'And it was detected by the defence, was it not?'

'Yes.'

'As having been altered?'

'Yes.'

'Altered in a way prejudicial to his evidence?'

'Yes.'

'Who had that passport? The police?'

'It was in my possession from the 7th November, when Lord Montagu gave it to me.'

Detective Superintendent Smith, who had arrested me, began his evidence. Peter Rawlinson stopped him, and asked if the jury could be sent out, as he proposed to lodge an objection. When the jury had gone, he asked the judge to rule inadmissible the statement which I had written at Scotland Yard, on the ground that it had been obtained 'on the promise of a favour given to him by Superintendent Jones, who suggested to him that it would be better for him to do this; that

75

he could not make any promise but that he would probably only be bound over'.

'Your Lordship will have already heard,' said Rawlinson, 'that at 8 a.m. he had asked to see a solicitor. I intend to call the solicitor, who attempted to get in touch with his client and who was, in fact, told that he could not at a certain time because his client was being charged, when the evidence will show that, in fact, that man was not charged until very much later that evening.

'In those circumstances, my Lord, in my submission that certainly is not a voluntary confession. I can say here and now that that statement is a statement on which a misinterpretation may well be put, as to certain of the phrases used therein.'

Superintendent Smith continued his evidence. He said that he had not heard Superintendent Jones make any promises or suggest that I should make a statement. He denied that he had told Mr Myers, my solicitor, that he could not come and see me immediately because I was being charged at that moment. He said it had not been 'convenient' for Mr Myers to come because he, Superintendent Smith of the Special Branch, had had 'a number of officers doing searches at different places'.

This was the first and only admission that the Special Branch was involved. On various other occasions Superintendent Smith was at great pains to explain that it was by pure chance that he had accompanied Jones to my house.

Smith agreed that, during the questioning, I had been in a very shocked and distraught condition. He had read my statement. 'It is the best statement I have ever seen written,' he said.

Superintendent Jones was a good deal tougher. He agreed that he had spent about three-and-a-half hours with me in the house, but vehemently denied having questioned me. It was not true, he said, that he had encouraged me to make a statement. If I said that, I was lying. He had read the statement.

'Were you moved by it, Mr Jones?'

'I wasn't moved; I thought it was a good statement.'

Mr Myers was then called. He said that he could have come to see me immediately, but that from his conversation with

Superintendent Smith he formed the impression that I was being charged at that moment, or was about to be charged. Mr Roberts, in cross-examination, asked: 'It may be that your recollection of the use of the word "charge" is imperfect?'

'I doubt it,' said Mr Myers.

I went into the witness box. It was painted pale grey, with a handrail to hold on to. Opposite me were the empty jury benches. I gave the judge the facts of my arrest, as I have given them here. Then Mr Roberts looked up at me and asked: 'You are, Mr Wildeblood, as your counsel has quite properly described you, an intelligent man?'

'I hope so.'

'And you knew perfectly well, when the police officers came that morning, that they were coming over on a very serious matter?'

'I did not appreciate the seriousness of it.'

'I suggest to you – you see, it has been described how very much upset you were; was not that because you realized the gravity of the situation?'

'I do not think so, sir.'

'Why were you upset, then?'

'If three police officers arrive at 8 o'clock on a very cold morning and start showing you letters you know you have written yourself, that you know would be extremely damaging if they were published, I think that is enough to upset anybody.'

'I quite agree with you; but would you now reconsider your answer to my question? My question was: you knew that they were coming over on a serious matter?'

'I knew it was a matter which would have a serious effect on my life, but I did not appreciate that in law it was so serious.'

'Did Superintendent Jones say "There is a warrant in existence for your arrest?"'

'No; if he had mentioned a warrant I should have asked to see it.'

When I had finished giving my evidence, the judge ruled that my statement was inadmissible, on the ground that it was not a voluntary statement.

By this time I had returned to the dock. A woman sitting on

the benches beside me leaned over the dock rail and grasped my arm.

'You'll be all right now,' she said, 'thank God.'

During the trial Arthur Prothero and I were staying at a small hotel just outside Winchester. It was strange, at breakfast time, to see the other residents reading newspapers with my own photograph on the front page. Wherever I went, there were Press cameramen. I knew most of them from my Fleet Street days. They would bob out of cars or doorways with their cameras held up, flattening the brims of their hats, and plead: 'Just a minute, please, Pete, do you mind?' But however many pictures they took, their Art Editors in London always seemed to print the old ones taken at Lymington during the preliminary hearing. It had been extremely cold at Lymington and my face, half-frozen, had acquired a tragic, hunted look which I suppose they thought appropriate.

Arthur Prothero realized that I did not look my best when I was suffering from the cold. He said to me: 'If you go into the witness box shivering like that you'll look as guilty as hell. Haven't you got any long pants?' I told him that I had not, so he lent me a pair of his own. There is some truth in the saying that a man's best friend is his solicitor.

The Court hearings lasted all day, and during the luncheon adjournment, Edward, Michael, and I went down to the cells below and unpacked a picnic lunch. This was sent over each day from Palace House, and invariably included half a bottle of wine. The cells were extremely small, and it was impossible to turn around without becoming covered with whitewash. They had barred windows and an atmosphere of antiquity and despair which reminded us strongly of the last act of *Tosca*. The warders were surprised and faintly scandalized when Michael began singing 'E lucevan le stelle' in a ringing baritone. We explored the other cells and found that in one of them the wall bore the text: 'Mister Justice So-and-so is a bottlenosed Old bastard who can't count, all he can say is Five, Seven, Nine years.' We discovered that the lavatory had no lock on the door and that the flush-plug was on the outside, presumably so that one could not hang oneself from the chain.

On the fourth day I gave my evidence. I was less nervous

this time than I had been during the hearing of the objection two days before, but I was obliged, on this occasion, to face the jury. It is most difficult to look twelve men straight in the eye at the same time.

The account of my life which I gave in the witness box was substantially the same, if less detailed, as that which I have given here. Mr Rawlinson questioned me about my feelings for McNally.

'I was extremely fond of him,' I said. 'I was grateful to him for his affection – which helped me in my loneliness – I was extremely lonely at that time. In a way, I suppose I enjoyed the company of somebody whom I thought I could help in various ways. As I said before, he was intelligent, but he wasn't educated; and I enjoyed showing him things and telling him things. I wasn't in love with him at that time, but it is very difficult, when somebody else is apparently in love with you, it is very difficult to resist expressing yourself in the same way that they do.'

I was asked about one of the letters, which Mr Roberts had described as 'breathing unnatural passion in almost every line' – a straight quotation, incidentally, from the trial of Oscar Wilde.

'I couldn't remember exactly what terms I had used, but I knew that I had said a lot of things in it that I didn't really mean, and that I had also said a lot of things that I shouldn't have said whether I meant them or not; so when we did meet again it was rather embarrassing, because my letter had put our relationship on a false basis, and to some extent a dangerous one,' I said.

Mr Roberts rose, hitched at his wig, poured out a teaspoonful of cough mixture and inquired: 'Have you any suggestion to put forward as to why McNally should tell, according to you, what are such wicked lies about you?'

'Yes, I should have thought the motive was perfectly obvious. He was either doing it to save his own skin or doing it to save somebody else's.'

'Save his own skin? How is he saving his own skin by saying what happened to you two?'

I thought this a remarkable question from the man who had

promised McNally complete immunity from prosecution, provided that he gave evidence against me. But Mr Rawlinson objected, so I was not given the chance of replying.

Then Mr Roberts began talking about homosexuals, inverts and perverts, in a sudden access of scientific zeal. One of the advantages of being cross-examined by Mr Roberts was that you could see his trick-questions coming a mile away, like flying bombs. I said: 'I think we all ought to agree on some kind of vocabulary. If I say somebody is a homosexual I am not necessarily implying that they indulge in criminal actions.'

Mr Roberts brushed this aside and went on talking about inverts and perverts. I knew what he was leading up to. He faced me squarely, peering up at me under his wig, and demanded: 'Your character has been put in at its highest, and I agree in every way – nothing has ever been brought against your character. You can hold your head high. But you are an invert?'

'Yes, I am an invert.'

I did not look at the jury to see what the result of this explosion had been. Mr Roberts was getting ready to launch his next bomb.

'It is a feature, is it not, that inverts or perverts seek their love associates in a different walk of life than their own?'

'I cannot accept that as a deduction. I have never heard any suggestion that that is the ordinary rule.'

'I mean, for instance, McNally was infinitely – he is none the worse for it – but infinitely your social inferior?'

'That is absolute nonsense.'

'Well, perhaps that is not a very polite way of answering my question.'

'I am sorry, I apologize.'

'Please do not apologize. I know very well you are under a great strain.'

'Nobody ever flung it at me during the War that I was associating with people who were infinitely my social inferiors.'

*

I was in the witness box for five hours. The task which Mr Roberts had set himself was to prove to the jury that the admittedly emotional relationship which had existed between McNally and myself could have only one basis: that of sexual desire. I pointed out that the letters, passionate or not, did not contain a single obscene phrase, nor one which could have been put in as evidence of sexual intercourse if the letters had been exchanged by a man and a woman. The whole of the prosecution case was built up on innuendo – a nightmare edifice of snobbery, deliberate ignorance, and hypocrisy based on the proposition: There's no smoke without fire.

Mr Schofield, the Editor of the *Daily Mail*, told the court that I had carried out my duties well, but that he had always considered me in appearance and manner 'rather effeminate'. Mr Schofield, I remembered, was extremely proud of his collection of fancy waistcoats; but he was not wearing one now.

Edward Montagu gave his evidence-in-chief loudly and precisely. He ended by describing his arrest, and the way in which he was prevented from seeing his solicitor.

Mr Roberts began his cross-examination by asking: 'Are you complaining about the police? You see, we have had a lot of questions from your learned counsel suggesting that there is some complaint to be made against the police. Are you making any complaint, Lord Montagu?'

'I think I have reason to.'

I watched the judge carefully. His face twitched with annoyance.

'Do you realize that the police have their duty to perform whether they are arresting Lord Montagu or Bill Sykes? You realize that, don't you?' asked Mr Roberts.

'I do.'

'And that there is no distinction whatever?'

' I hope not.'

Edward Montagu then proceeded to deny, in detail, the charges against him.

'Would you like to say,' inquired Mr Roberts, 'if you have any idea, why this airman should make such a wicked invention against you?'

'Well, I think the best answer would perhaps be found in something that I heard Reynolds say before the magistrates at Lymington.'

'Yes?'

'To the effect that he was so terrified that he was prepared to answer "yes" to anything that was put to him; that he had given up hope — '

'Who terrified him then?'

' — and that he did not know how much to say in order to please them.'

'Who terrified him?'

Edward smiled. 'I wasn't there,' he said.

*

Michael Pitt-Rivers was half-way through his evidence-in-chief when the court adjourned for the week-end. I went home to my mother and father. We had not expected the case to go on for so long, and funds were beginning to run low again.

When I got back to the hotel at Winchester on Sunday night I learned from the reporters that my house in London had been burgled. I telephoned a friend in Chelsea who went to the house and reported that nothing of value seemed to have been taken, but that the intruder had searched through all my papers, flinging them about as though he was looking for something. The same thing had happened a few days earlier at Palace House, Edward's home. Later, we discovered that the only things which had been taken were a wireless set and a suitcase. The police set about taking finger-prints and posted a guard on the house. It amused me to think that most of the finger-prints on my furniture would be found to be those of Superintendent Jones and Superintendent Smith.

The next morning the main headline in the *Daily Mirror* announced, in letters two inches high: 'WILDEBLOOD'S HOUSE RAIDED.' I had ousted the Mau Mau, McCarthy, and even a pair of Siamese twins from the front page.

*

On the sixth day, Mr Roberts made his closing speech to the jury. It began with a refrain which had become monotonous: the police, whatever they had done, were only doing their duty. The police were perfectly right to search the flats without a warrant, the refusal to allow the accused men to see their solicitors was 'an ordinary precaution', and it was extremely unkind to describe Inspector Stuchfield as a 'Peeping Tom', even if he did read all Lord Montagu's letters from his fiancée. Furthermore, if the police had done anything wrong, it was not a matter for the jury. What they had to do was to decide the case on the facts.

Mr Roberts, rather strangely, complained of the ardour of the defence. He said that 'every stone, every shell, every insult' had been hurled at McNally. This seemed to goad Mr Roberts into a frenzy; perhaps because he feared that a valuable piece of Crown property had been damaged by the bombardment. Innuendo gave way to sheer, frantic invention. I had by now become 'an obvious homosexual', the cider had turned into champagne again, and a perfectly orthodox photograph of Reynolds in bathing-trunks was described, with relish, as 'a somewhat sexual photograph' – whatever that may mean.

Mr Roberts ended by saying: 'Members of the jury, I am sure that if I have over-presented this case, over-pressed it in any way, you will stand as the guardians, the representatives of safety, between the prosecution and the possibility of an injustice. You will listen most carefully, of course, to my learned friends before you have the privilege of listening to my Lord's summing-up.' He pulled the folds of his gown tight across his stomach, with a satisfied air. 'I can only submit,' he said, 'that dreadful and sordid as was the story that these two young men had to tell, it is amply borne out by the circumstances and shown to be the true one. The only crime they have committed meriting this interrogation – properly administered by my learned friends – is the fact that they have told the truth.'

He sat down, pulled his bottle of cough-mixture towards him, and found to his annoyance that it was empty.

*

Peter Rawlinson began his final speech by picking up Mr Roberts' reference to 'this sordid tale'. 'Of course it is an ugly, sordid tale,' he said. 'But for the personalities engaged in it, what interest would any normal human being have in it? My Lord is here for the duty he has to do; *you* are; so are counsel; so are witnesses; so are the police. One wonders, indeed, that

83

people should queue up and listen, to come here and see what they did when Wildeblood was giving evidence – the crucifixion of a human being, as he explained to you what he feels within himself, how he is moved and how he has behaved. This is something which you have had to see, which my Lord has had to see, those people engaged in the case have had to see. You may think it strange that people should want to come and watch it.'

'You are not concerned, members of the jury,' he went on, 'whether a trial such as this, on charges such as this, is a happy reflection upon our state of civilization. You are not concerned about the merits of the law. None of us are.' The question before the jury was: who is telling the truth?

'My friend (Mr Roberts) with his rhetoric and with his great experience poured such scorn, did he not, on the sad, miserable story that Wildeblood has told us as to his relationship, his feelings, for this person who now turns out with the character that he has.

'My friend used his great gifts again on this matter of the social inferiority. You remember Wildeblood's answer: that nobody flung that at him when he was an Aircraftman serving in the war? What social inferiority? What has that to do with it?'

Mr Rawlinson then turned to the manner in which the case had been brought. The RAF investigation disclosed that McNally had committed offences with several men in Cambridgeshire and London. 'Why, then, should the RAF send for the Hampshire police? Why? Why? Why?

'You remember what was written in those letters. You may remember that there was that mention of the magic word, "Beaulieu". You may think that started off the train which has ended here in this trial before you.'

He described the handing-over of the case by the RAF police to Superintendent Jones, the mock trial, the continual interrogations of McNally.

'We have suggested all through this case, members of the jury, that there was this inducement to this man to tell lies. If ever a witness had an inducement to tell lies, didn't he have it? Knowing they were investigating homosexuality, knowing that he was a homosexual, knowing the term of imprisonment that he was likely to serve, what better thing could he do than fling some mud in the right direction, and to throw it at the person in whom they were most interested – Peter Wildeblood, the Diplomatic Correspondent of a London newspaper?

'Why should it not be suggested, therefore, by the defence, that McNally had every reason to tell some lies as to that relationship?

'That this law, such as it is, does contain within itself the seeds of blackmail, everybody acknowledges and knows. Whether we approve of that or not, as I have said before, is not the concern of any of us here in this trial; but I did ask McNally: why did he keep that letter which was written by Wildeblood? I asked him if he thought it would be of any use.

'Well, it has been of use to him. If he had not got those letters, then this inquiry might not have proceeded; he might not have been given the assurance, as he was by my learned friend, that he was not going to be prosecuted. He might have been facing serious charges and terms of imprisonment – if he had not had that letter.'

Having described McNally's motive for lying, Mr Rawlinson proceeded to examine his evidence in detail, pointing out a number of inconsistencies. Then:

'Wildeblood gave his evidence; and I suggest to you that he gave his evidence with the sincerity, truthfulness, and frankness of few witnesses. My learned friend, who now brushes aside all this business about "invert", "pervert" and "homosexual" in his speech — ' (Mr Roberts had given up being scientific in these matters and had used the three words indiscriminately, explaining that he 'was not well up in these subtle distinctions') ' — my learned friend was most careful to ask Mr Wildeblood whether he was an invert or a pervert and what it meant, and insisted that he answer the question, and Wildeblood's answer was "Yes, I am an invert."

' "Yes, I am one of those unfortunate creatures who have within them that desire, that attraction towards another male person, and not the ordinary, normal desire of an ordinary, normal human being."

85

'Members of the jury, those of us who are fortunate enough to have ordinary, normal lives can afford to look at that kind of thing so much more justly, with so much greater pity, than those persons who, for some reason – perhaps that they themselves are not always normal – always adopt an attitude of protesting, perhaps, a little too much.

'As you saw him there you must have felt some sympathy, and felt that he was telling my learned friend all he could about this relationship which had ended in his standing there in the dock. His attitude to McNally was one of emotional fondness for him, a person who could supply him with company in his loneliness. All he had with this man – who, we now know, was having a physical relationship with some other man somewhere else on these other week-ends – was this emotional relationship.

'Almost enough to make you snigger, is it not? Almost enough to make anybody laugh, a story such as that. My friend pours scorn upon it and says: "Can you possibly believe that there was no sexual relationship between those two persons?" Is it so impossible? Does it mean that every time a man and a woman exchange love letters or stay in each other's company, that there is a sexual relationship between them? That is really what it amounts to, isn't it – that you have to assume a sexual relationship because of the fact that on six occasions they were in each other's company for a week-end, spent a holiday of seven nights together; and one passionate love letter was written by Wildeblood to that man McNally.'

He read the letters which McNally had received from the man Gerry, a male nurse. ' "After all, as you realize, it only needs a letter to the General Nursing Council to ruin me; that is the reason for my extreme caution, and please don't keep this letter!"

'And,' said Rawlinson, 'Master McNally, of course, tucks it away carefully. . . . Now, is it not understandable that we should accuse him of keeping things for his own use? Is it not understandable that he is a totally unreliable man, not only morally but as a witness of truth? And I therefore suggest to you that he is not a person upon whom you can rely.

'I would refer you, once again, to the misfortune of the man

86

Peter Wildeblood. If you had to choose between those witnesses as to who was telling the truth and who was being sincere, is it not quite obvious that when Wildeblood stood there in that box, he was telling the truth – that he was the man upon whom the whole burden of this trial really rested, that, as an invert, he is the mainstream through which the whole course of this trial really runs?

'That man is in your hands. If you convict him, you convict him on the evidence of Edward McNally. The matters of corroboration also corroborate his own story, of an emotional feeling, and an emotional love, for this man Edward McNally. You will convict, if you should convict, purely on the evidence of a man who has already been shown to be a liar, and utterly unreliable on all points.

'My friend has said you will not be moved by sympathy, and you will not be moved by pity. Wildeblood does not ask you for pity. He does not ask you for sympathy. Whatever happens in this trial, he must face a desperate future. All he does ask you for, and what I ask you for in his case, is justice.'

*

That night, a woman spat at me. She was a respectable-looking, middle-aged, tweedy person wearing a sensible felt hat. She was standing on the pavement as the car went by. I saw her suck in her cheeks, and the next moment a big blob of spit was running down the windscreen.

This shocked me very much. The woman did not look eccentric or evil; in fact she looked very much like the country gentlewomen with whom my mother used to take coffee when she had finished her shopping on Saturday mornings. She looked thoroughly ordinary, to me. But what did I look like to her? Evidently, I was a monster. I was quite sure that she had never spat at anyone in her life before. And yet, she had hated me enough to do this.

I began to think. I did not believe that I deserved to be spat at; but, if people could be so wrong about me, was it not also possible that I had wrong ideas about other people? Mr Roberts, for example; I began to think about Mr Roberts.

So far, in this account of the trial, I have presented Mr

Roberts as something of a grotesque, which is how he appeared to me at the time. My feelings towards him now began to change. I remembered how he had passionately defended Rupert Croft-Cooke. Had he been sincere in that trial, or in this? Or in both? Or in neither?

I had seen a great deal of barristers by now. I realized that their profession was closely akin to that of actors, and that insincerity was the stock-in-trade of most of them. But how could they be sincere, alternating as they did between Crown and defence, knowing the tricks of both sides? It would be as unreasonable to expect sincerity from a prostitute. Year in, year out, these men stood, now on one side, now on the other, pleading the cause of Crown and criminal with equal vehemence. At the end of a long career at the Bar they must have become like stones, washed clean of all sympathy, all hope for humanity, all regard for truth – and it was then, by a singular stroke of irony, that they were made into judges.

No, I could not hate Mr Roberts, because I did not know him. I only knew what he had said in court, and I could not hate him for that because he probably believed it no more than I did. He was probably not even a snob. I had met his wife, and she had been a kindly, matey soul who would be the last person in the world to rant about social superiorities. As a matter of fact she had bought me several gins, to cheer me up. Mr Roberts, I decided, was as much a victim of hypocrisy as I was myself. It was his job to secure a conviction under a law of which, for all I knew, he disapproved as strongly as myself. He was doing his job. If he did it well, I would go to prison.

I was too tired to think about prison. I reflected that warders were probably only people, like anybody else, and went to sleep.

*

The seventh day began with the closing speech of Mr Fearnley-Whittingstall, in defence of Lord Montagu. Peter Rawlinson's speech had been fiery and moving, like the speech of a man defending the honour of a friend. Fearnley-Whittingstall's was delivered more coldly, more oratorically, but it was obvious that he, too, felt strongly about the victimization of his client. He spoke first of the Boy Scout case, in which he had also defended Edward.

He reminded the jury that Edward had already been awaiting a re-trial when he was arrested on January 9th – 'long before you knew that you would be jurymen in the case. I wonder how many of you said to yourself: "How on earth can that wretched man get an unprejudiced trial now?"

'My learned friend has said several times during the course of this case: "There is no reason, is there, Lord Montagu, why Lord Montagu should be treated any differently from Bill Sykes?" And you remember Lord Montagu's reply: "I hope not."

'I do not know and cannot think of any occasion when a situation equal to the one which you are faced with has happened before – that a 20-months-old association has been made the subject-matter of a trial intervening between the trial in December and the other trial.'

Mr Fearnley-Whittingstall argued that there was no reason to suppose that Lord Montagu knew that I was an invert, as I now admitted. 'That is the kind of thing that a person keeps closely to himself, and does not tell his intimate friends.

'Mr Roberts has said that Wildeblood was obviously a homosexual. That is in conflict with the evidence; it is in conflict with Wildeblood's career, which has been a highly successful one.

'Do you suppose that in a place like Fleet Street, if Wildeblood was an obvious homosexual, as Mr Roberts has held him out to be, it would not have gained currency, gossip, rumour, and carried itself to the ears of Wildeblood's superiors upon the paper?'

This was, of course, perfectly true. I had always managed to keep my tendencies hidden from all my friends in Fleet Street; not so much because I was ashamed of them, but because they were none of their business.

Then Mr Fearnley-Whittingstall turned to the question of the 'lavish hospitality'. 'Lavish hospitality! It looks fine, does it not, when you get a peer and a successful journalist, to talk about lavish hospitality. Not quite so fine when you examine the facts. From the point of view of Lord Montagu, a loaf of bread and some champagne cider. From the point of view of Wildeblood, eggs for an omelette and a few slices of salami. Lavish hospitality!'

Mr Hylton-Foster, making his closing speech on behalf of Michael Pitt-Rivers, was even more jocose. 'Foreigners think we are a nation of snobs,' he remarked. 'Well, I think we are. But you must have got some pretty basic snobbery in this case. It is now said that because on a sunshiny holiday, with chaps in beach clothes down in a beach hut, in those circumstances when they are all calling one another by their Christian names, you let them call you by your Christian name, that is a badge of some indecent association. Really! Did ever snobbery put forward a more greasy exterior than that by the prosecution in this case?'

Mr Hylton-Foster said it had been suggested that the airmen were lying to save their own skin. He did not know whether this was true; he could only point out that Reynolds had saved his.

*

On the night before, the Press men had been laying odds of eleven to two that we should be acquitted. The odds must have slumped heavily after they had heard the first half of the judge's summing-up.

Mr Justice Ormerod leaned forward from his throne and spoke to the jury in a voice so rapid and low that we, at the other end of the court, could scarcely hear it. He warned them of the dangers of accepting the evidence of accomplices, but remarked, very truly, that 'it would be extremely difficult to launch a prosecution in a case of this kind if it were not possible to obtain evidence of this kind'.

He repeated the case for the prosecution, putting it rather better, I thought, than Mr Roberts. Then he considered the criticisms which had been made of the police.

'You will remember in this case,' said the judge, 'that the police have their duty to do. Of course you are not concerned with the question, which may or may not be a difficult question of law, as to whether the police had any right to search the flat of Lord Montagu or the flat of Major Pitt-Rivers in London.

You may well understand that the police were anxious to effect simultaneous arrests of these three men; anxious, perhaps, that they could do that in order that they could search the premises, in case any relevant documents were destroyed or got rid of in one way or another; and you may think it reasonable that the police should act as they did, arrest these men early in the morning, and at the same time search their premises, and, when they were satisfied the three men had been arrested, allow these men to get in touch with their solicitors. . . . '

The jury, of course, did not know that I had been prevented from seeing my solicitor for five hours after my arrest. Mr Justice Ormerod did.

*

That evening I was very depressed. Arthur Prothero said: 'Naturally, it sounded bad. He was just re-stating the prosecution case. To-morrow he'll put the defence case, and the jury will have it fresh in their minds when they retire.' I was not convinced. 'He sounded as though his heart was in it,' I said.

We went to a hotel to have a drink with some of the reporters. They asked whether there would be a party if we were acquitted.

'Look here,' I said, 'I don't want any of your corny stories.'

'What corny stories, Pete?'

'I don't want to wake up in prison on Thursday morning and read a story about a "little grey-haired bottle of champagne sat waiting last night. . . ." '

'Oh, you aren't going to prison. We'll help you to drink the champagne.'

'I'll settle for champagne cider.'

'No, really, what will you do? If everything goes all right, I mean?'

'Go to Winchester Cathedral and get down on my knees.' I was quite serious about it.

'That'll make a smashing picture. Can I have it exclusive?'

I saw Superintendent Smith on the other side of the bar. I walked over and bought him a gin and tonic. 'I hope they won't arrest you for that burglary at my house,' I said.

Smith grinned. 'Why should they?'

'Your finger-prints are all over everything. Cheers.'

'Good luck,' he said.

I reflected that, under different circumstances, I might have made a friend of Smith. He reminded me of Bob Fabian, the Scotland Yard detective now retired, with whom I had dined a few nights before the trial began. Fabian, too, had wished me luck. How ridiculous it all was! To-morrow the jury would give their verdict. It was quite possible that I would go to prison. And what would that prove? Officially, that I was an enemy of Society, a criminal. The newspapers would brand me as such; it was their duty. Smith would probably be promoted for his part in tracking me down. Roberts would be congratulated by the Director of Public Prosecutions. Reynolds and McNally would go free. It was like a game of consequences. And the world said. . . .

One of the photographers, hidden behind the bar, was snapping me with a Leica. A reporter was asking whether I had thought of writing my life story for the Sunday papers. I thought it was time to go to bed.

*

In the morning, Wednesday morning, March 24th, I packed the clothes I was not wearing and handed th..m, together with the borrowed underpants, to Arthur Prothero. I arranged that either he or one of the reporters, Peter Drake of the *Daily Express*, should telephone the verdict to my parents.

The judge continued his summing-up. He put forward the case for the defence, but as each point arose he reminded the jury of the Crown allegations. He had obviously been horrified by my admission that I was a sexual invert, and annoyed by the criticism of the police; his whole exposition was subtly coloured by these two considerations. My letters were 'nauseating'. The judge remarked, of one passage: 'Of course, that is an extraordinary phrase for one man to write to another; but you will remember that it is a letter written from a man who is admittedly homosexual to a man who, whether Wildeblood knew it at the time, or not, we now know was a homosexual too, and you will have to consider the letter of course in relation to those circumstances.'

I remembered my own words: 'I think we ought to agree on some kind of vocabulary. If I say somebody is a homosexual I am not necessarily implying that they indulge in criminal actions.'

I remembered the words of the Church of England report: 'It should be recognized that homosexual love is not always at a genital level. The homosexual is capable of a virtuous love as clean, as decent and as beautiful as one who is normally sexed.'

At five minutes past twelve the jury retired to consider their verdict.

*

Arthur Prothero came down to the cells. 'I'm sorry, Peter,' he said. 'We've had it. You've got to face that now.'

'Are there any grounds for appeal?' I asked.

'I'm afraid not. There were no actual misdirections, in law.'

'I see.'

We had lunch, as usual, in the cells. Afterwards I went and looked for one of the warders, to whom I had spoken several times. I found him sitting on a bench in the corridor, drinking a cup of tea.

'My solicitor thinks I've had it,' I said.

'Oh, don't say that yet. You never know, with juries.'

'I know with this one. What's prison like?'

He laughed. 'Not too bad; if you've been in the forces you'll know what to expect.'

'I suppose the food's pretty awful.'

'Well, it's plain, of course, but there's plenty of it. Most chaps put on a bit of weight inside, as a matter of fact. It's probably the starch. Anyhow, let's hope you don't find out.'

I noted that he had stopped calling me 'Sir'. He had always done so, up to now. I supposed that I should be calling him 'Sir', to-morrow.

It was half past two.

Another case had begun. The accused man was a round-faced Irishman, charged with murder. I could hear the

93

machine of justice grinding away as we sat, hour after hour, waiting for the verdict. I had no doubt what it would be. The judge had explained the probabilities clearly enough: anybody who admitted to being a homosexual was so vile, so obscene that the chances were that he was a criminal as well. I waited with a dull curiosity for his sentence. He could put me in prison for 15 years, if he felt so disposed.

At last – it was half past four – the jury came back. The other case was brusquely suspended, and Montagu, Pitt-Rivers, and I were hustled up the stairs and into the dock for the last time.

I heard the foreman of the jury say: 'Guilty. . . . Guilty. . . . Guilty. . . . Not Guilty.' They had found me not guilty of one of the offences which McNally had alleged; they had decided that the principal witness for the Crown was lying; but what did it matter? 'Guilty. . . . Guilty. . . . Guilty. . . . ' There's no smoke without fire.

We had one more witness. Dr Jack Hobson, a psychiatrist at the Middlesex Hospital whom I had seen for a week before the trial, told the judge that he believed I had suicidal tendencies as well as being sexually abnormal. He believed my homosexuality could be cured, but it would be more difficult to do this if I was sent to prison.

Peter Rawlinson pleaded with the judge. 'Wildeblood's is a medical problem,' he said, 'a problem which must be solved, if a man as worthwhile as he is is not to be thrown away on the rubbish-heap of humanity.' He said that I had been convicted on the evidence of rotten, worthless, miserable creatures. I had not corrupted them – I had never corrupted anybody. 'Perhaps the greatest prerogative of a judge is that of mercy,' he declared. 'If ever a man needed your mercy, that man is Peter Wildeblood.'

After the other two counsel for the defence had spoken, the judge asked us if we had anything to say.

'I have nothing to say,' I said.

'Nothing to say.'

'Nothing.'

The judge straightened his back. 'You have all three been found guilty of serious offences,' he said. 'You Montagu, of less serious offences than the other two. I have paid the greatest attention to everything that has been said on your behalf, and particular attention, Wildeblood, to the difficulties which you have, no doubt, encountered.

'But, of course, it is quite impossible for these offences to be passed over. I am dealing with you in the most lenient way that I possibly can. You, Wildeblood, will go to prison for 18 months; you, Montagu, for 12 months; and you, Pitt-Rivers, for 18 months.'

The warders stepped forward and hurried us down the stairs. I just had time for a last look at McNally, sitting between Superintendent Jones and another policeman. He was staring straight ahead. I took a deep breath, as though I were diving.

The warder to whom I had spoken before was waiting for me. 'You'll only do 12 months, if you behave yourself,' he told me, 'and of course you will. Just remember: there's always somebody else who's worse off than you.'

'Thank you, Sir,' I said.

＊

Peter Drake telephoned my mother and told her the news. He read her a message which I had written earlier that afternoon. 'The jury are out now,' I had said. 'Whatever they decide, I do not want you to be ashamed of anything I have done. Be glad, rather, that at last a little light has been cast on this dark territory in which, through no fault of their own, many thousands of other men are condemned to live, in loneliness and fear.'

The reporters agreed that they would not trouble my mother any further. She released a statement to the Press: 'I have never lost faith in my son. The sentence does not change anything.' Then she sat down and wept.

Next morning we were taken to work in the mail-bag shop, where we had our first chance of meeting the other prisoners. Since there was only one workshop at Winchester, it contained all kinds of convicts: the 'Stars' or first offenders, the 'Ordinaries' who had been in prison before, and 'Debtors' wearing brown coats to distinguish them from the convicted men.

Sitting slightly apart from the rest, with blue and white patches sewn on their suits, were the men who had tried to escape. They sewed the mail-bags, while the rest of us folded the canvas, cut the ropes into lengths, ripped up the worn-out bags and stitched metal rings on to the tabs. The debtors sat in a cloud of dust, unpicking a matted heap of coir fibre and stuffing it into mattresses.

An instructor explained what we were to do. My first job was waxing the mail-bag thread with a mixture of beeswax and lamp black; later I graduated to the table where the canvas was folded into the appropriate shapes. Two bored warders sat watching us to see that we got on with the work and did not talk. In spite of this, an extraordinary amount of communication took place by means of whispers, gestures, and winks. I never realized before how much a wink could convey.

'Sleep O.K.?'

'Not too bad, thanks.'

Fold top, fold side, fold in half.

'You'll get used to it. Not bad here, really.'

'What are the warders like?'

'Screws, we call them. Some of them are pigs. That one over there, for instance. Proper sadist.'

'What does he do?'

Fold top, fold side, fold in half.

'Eats sweets, for one thing. Unwraps them as slowly as he can, and then pops them into his gate, all gloating like. Careful, he's watching you.'

Fold top, fold side, fold in half.

'What are you in for, or doesn't one ask?'

'That's all right, mate. Mutiny.'

'Oh.'

'Me and my oppo was in the Royal Navy, see, and one day we got a bit choked with the Master-at-Arms. . . . Careful.'

Fold top, fold side, fold in half. The warder's eyes, pale blue under his peaked cap, swivelled slowly to the far side of the room, where a Jamaican stowaway was humming to himself a little too loudly.

'So, being full of several rum rations, I tapped him on the nut. Didn't know what I was doing, really.'

'And what did you get?'

'Twelve years.'

Fold, fold, fold. There's always someone worse off than you.

'I wonder what time it is?'

'Soon find out. Psst, Ginger!'

A cadaverous youth sitting by the window looked up. The mutineer raised his hand to chest-level, turned his wrist and examined the place where his watch would have been. Ginger got up and looked out of the window to some distant clock.

'Hey, you! Sit down!'

'Yes, sir.'

'What d'you want to know the time for? You've got plenty of time, haven't you?'

'Yes, sir.'

'Then don't let me see you looking out of that window again, or I'll have your guts for garters.'

'Yes, sir.'

Stitch, stitch, stitch. Fold, fold, fold. After a minute or two Ginger looked up and silently mouthed the words: twenty past ten.

'Twenty past ten.'

'Is that all?'

Fold top . . . fold side . . . fold in half. . . .

Winchester Prison is a star-shaped building of red brick, looking as though it had been carved out of carbolic soap. Each arm of the star is a block of cells, comprising three landings connected by iron staircases and observation bridges. The spaces between the landings are covered with wire netting to discourage suicides. The corners between the cell-blocks are filled in with exercise yards and a few flowerbeds, and the whole building is surrounded by a high brick wall.

I was summoned to an interview by the Reception Board,

which consisted of the Governor, the Chaplain, and several other officials. The Governor did most of the talking. He was a middle-aged man with a kindly air and a head covered in sprightly grey curls. I was told to sit down.

'Have you given any thought,' the Governor asked, 'to what you will do when you have completed your sentence?'

'Yes,' I said, 'I shall go on writing.'

He put his head on one side. 'But not, of course, under your own name?'

'I don't see why not, sir.'

'Well, you may find it a little more difficult than you imagine. Have you considered going to live abroad? People in your position often do, you know.'

'If you will excuse me for saying so, sir, I think that would be a most cowardly course.'

'Yes? Now tell me – do you believe in God?'

I hesitated. The Governor continued: 'You see, if we can find out where you stand in that matter perhaps we shall be able to – er – sort you out in other ways.' He looked under his eyebrows at the Chaplain, who fixed me with an interested stare.

'Yes, I believe in God. But not the God of any of the organized religions. I believe there is something good in each one of us, and I suppose you could call that God.'

'Don't you practise any religion, then?'

'No, sir. I think most of them have something to recommend them, but none of them has convinced me that it holds a monopoly of the truth.'

'I see,' said the Governor triumphantly. 'So what you are doing is trying to find a religion that fits in with your own code of behaviour; isn't that it?'

'Certainly not,' I replied, stung. 'If that were so I should have picked on the Church of England, which has shown a great deal more tolerance and understanding towards people like me than any other church I know of.'

'Really?'

The Chaplain's lips moved, but he was evidently not meant to interrupt while the Governor was assessing a prisoner's character. I wondered what the Governor was going to write about me: 'truculent and aggressive,' probably – but I hadn't meant to be.

'The Church of England Moral Welfare Council ...' I began, but the Governor was looking at me testily. He did not seem to have heard of the Report, or at least did not wish to discuss it. 'I see from your record that you have said you would be willing to undergo medical treatment.'

'Yes, sir, if any is available.'

'You will see the Medical Officer in due course.'

*

The Medical Officer was a hard-bitten little Scot with grey hair brushed into a schoolboyish bang. He had been a prison doctor at Brixton for many years. He asked me how I was feeling, listened to my heartbeats, told me to sit down and began firing off the usual psychiatrist's questions, writing down my replies. Since my private life was now public property, I spoke frankly of my childhood and adolescence, while he grunted occasionally and his pen raced over the paper.

'You say you know a lot of other homosexuals. Tell me, do you frequent the orgies in which they indulge?'

'Orgies?'

'Yes, I believe in Chelsea and places there are houses where male and female homosexuals congregate to carry out unnatural practices together.'

'Do they? It sounds most unlikely to me.'

'So I am told.'

If he has been a prison doctor for so long, I thought, possibly he knows more about it than I do.

'Homosexuals do have meeting-places, of course,' I said, 'but they are usually quite respectable.'

'What sort of places?'

'Oh, public-houses mostly. There's one in almost every district of London.'

'Really? Is that so? I've never heard of that.' In that case, I thought, you are singularly ill-informed.

'Have you any hobbies?'

'Yes, plenty. Gardening, going to the theatre, cooking, painting. . . .'

'But no sport? No golf or tennis, for instance?'

'No.'

'And what,' he asked, 'do you do on your free evenings? Go out importuning?'

I could have hit him.

'Certainly not. I don't do that sort of thing. In any case, I haven't got the time. I only have one free evening a week, and I usually spend that with friends.'

'Other homosexuals, of course?'

And so on.

*

The getting-up bell rang at 6.30 every morning. By 7 o'clock we were supposed to have our cells tidy and our beds made up in the approved manner, leaning against the wall with the bedding hanging over them, blanket-sheet-blanket-sheet-blanket, with the hems in line. Then our cells were un-locked, a razor blade was issued to each man, and after a quick shave in cold water we trooped out on to the landing for the ritual of Slopping Out.

There was one flush-toilet and one sink for every twenty cells on the landing, and one cold water tap. At each of these points, known collectively as Recesses, stood a queue of prisoners in various stages of undress, waiting to refill their jugs and pour the contents of wash-basin and chamber-pot down the drain. The general effect, with three landings in view, was rather like some curious Neapolitan slum in which all the domestic chores were being done by men.

Carrying my chamber-pot self-consciously before me, I walked towards the recess. A voice behind me said:

'You're carrying that goddam pot as though it was the Holy Sacrament or something.'

'Well, it isn't. It's the Holy Excrement.'

'There's a pretty unholy smell around here. Why can't those guys get a move on?'

'Have you been in long?'

'Not here. I've just come from a London prison named Wandsworth. And before that I did four years in Sing-Sing.'

'Are you from the States?'

'No, I'm Canadian.'

'What was Sing-Sing like?'

'It was a cinch, beside this. Hell, they let me write short stories there, and sell them, too.'

'I'm a writer as well.'

'Go on? We must compare manuscripts. I've got permission to do a novel. I'll dump the notebooks in your cell when we slop out on Saturday; there's less chance of a search at the week-end. Come on, you're missing your turn. See you to-morrow.'

It was not, I discovered, considered very polite to ask another prisoner what he was 'in' for. One usually found out soon enough. In my case, there was no need for anyone to ask. Everyone in the prison, apparently, had been following the trial with the most searching interest.

'What I'd like to see,' remarked one of the burglars, 'is them two airmen coming in here. They wouldn't half get a good hiding.'

'Not a chance,' I said. 'They're quite safe.'

'Well, I'd like to see it, all the same. Cor, the Law didn't half take a diabolical liberty with you. Why didn't you get it stopped?'

'I didn't have a chance.'

'Come off it. A nice bit of dropsy to a copper usually does the trick. "Why, constable," you says' – and his voice took on the accents of Kensington – ' "there must be some mistake!" And you drops a bundle of ready on the table, all nonchalant-like.'

'Yes, perhaps. I never thought of it.'

'That's the trouble with you blokes. Ain't been properly brought up. I bet they tried to make you write a statement, too.'

'Yes.'

'Christ, it makes my heart bleed. Well, you'll know better next time, won't you?'

*

The official regulations allow a prisoner to write, and receive an answer to, one letter every two weeks. A good many of my friends did not know about this rule, and accordingly wrote to me. I was not allowed to read these letters, but whenever they arrived – which was almost every day – the Governor called me before him.

This 'call-up' entailed waiting outside the Governor's office for anything up to an hour and a half. The prisoners were supposed to stand several feet apart, and were not permitted to talk to each other. As usual, we managed to ignore this rule.

One day I stood next to a thin, dark man with a slight Australian accent, who had been imprisoned for the theft of some jewellery. He asked me whether I was going to write a book about prison life. I said I probably would, some day. At this, I heard a shuffling sound behind me and realized that another prisoner was listening to the conversation, and edging up on me.

'You can put this in your book,' he hissed. 'There's needles in the soup.'

'Needles?'

'Yes, bloody great darning needles. I'm writing to my MP about it.'

'Don't take any notice,' said the jewel thief. 'He's as nutty as a fruit-cake.'

'Shut your trap, or I'll do you. It's true, Mr Wildeblood, honest it is. I've got one in me now, long as your little finger.'

'Have you seen the MO?' I asked.

'Yes, but d'you know what? He refuses to X-ray me. Refuses. So I goes to the Governor every morning to lodge an official complaint.'

'Do you admire Oscar Wilde?' asked the jewel thief, hoping to cut the other prisoner out of the conversation.

'As a writer, yes,' I said. 'As a man, no. I think he did every-thing wrong. He shouldn't have let his friends persuade him to leave England when he came out. He should have shown a bit more guts.'

'Yes, but I suppose it was more difficult in those days. As a matter of fact, I came across rather a good phrase of his the other day, about his trial and everything. He said the hue and cry against him was "the rage of Caliban, on seeing his own face reflected in the glass". It's very true, I think. It's always the people who have a queer streak of their own who make the most violent attacks upon us.'

'Us?'

'Yes; us.'

'But I thought . . . '

'Oh, but the place is *packed* with gay people who are in for something else. Most of the screaming pansies are in for receiving, actually. Don't have anything to do with them, they're absolute hell, all having affairs with the Officers and bitching everybody like mad.'

'Thanks, I won't.'

'Lots of bloody grasses,' said the man with the stomach full of needles.

'Oh dear,' said the Australian, 'are you still here? I hoped you'd dropped dead.'

'What are grasses?' I asked.

'Informers. Short for "grasshoppers", which is rhyming slang for "shoppers", meaning people who go to the cop-shop and squeal on their friends.'

'Shut up!' yelled a warder. 'Get ready for the Governor!'

When my turn came, I was told to stand with my toes touching a line painted on the floor of the Governor's office. '8505, Peter Wildeblood, Sir,' I said.

The Governor looked up from his desk. A brown trilby hat was perched incongruously on his rakish grey curls. He smiled.

'Ah yes, Wildeblood. Do you know someone who might sign themselves "Mrs Massey"?' He had a letter in front of him. I thought for a moment. 'No, sir, I don't think I know a Mrs Massey. I know a Mr Massie. . . . '

'Aha!'

I wondered why Henry Massie, a reporter who worked for the *Daily Mail*, should be 'aha!'

'Or perhaps,' suggested the Governor, 'perhaps you recognize this – this person's, er, professional name, which appears to be . . . ' He read out the name of a girl reporter on the Press Association, which I recognized at once. I had forgotten her married name was Massey.

'Oh yes, sir, I know her.'

The Governor appeared to be disappointed, for some

reason. He took up another letter. 'And do you know anyone who might sign themselves "Iris"?'

'Yes, sir, I know three Irises.'

'It seems to be quite a common name in your – ah – circles,' twinkled the Governor. 'You will not, of course, be allowed either of these letters, since they are superfluous to your entitlement. They will be put in your Property, for you to read when you are released.'

'Thank you, sir.' I turned and went out. Outside the door, the truth hit me like a brick. The Governor thought those letters were from men.

*

There were three distinct types of homosexuals in the prison. First there were the genuine glandular cases, the men who were in fact women in everything but body. As my Australian friend had said, they had often been sent to prison for crimes quite unconnected with sex. They ran riot in the gaol. Since they were not officially 'sex cases', they were frequently put with other prisoners, three to a cell. They addressed each other by girls' names, flirted with the warders, and even managed to acquire perfume and make-up. I thought them rather revolting, but it was quite obvious that most of them could not help being what they were. Their outrageous behaviour was simply their way of making the best of things. They enjoyed attracting attention, and they had never had such a good opportunity.

Secondly, there were the men who had been sent to prison for seducing small boys. These were not popular with the other prisoners, although, curiously enough, they came in for rather less condemnation than the men whose sex-crimes had involved young girls. This may have been because their sentences were generally far heavier. It was impossible not to pity them, however much one disapproved of them.

Thirdly, there were the men like myself, who had been convicted of crimes with other adults. There did not seem to be any discrimination against them by other prisoners. The general attitude was: 'If someone wants to do that sort of thing, it's their own business.' At Winchester, many of these men had been sent to prison as the result of army or naval courts-martial. They were not in any way effeminate or 'obvious', and they disapproved as much as I did of the two groups I have already mentioned. In addition to them, there was quite a large number of men of the same type who were in prison for other kinds of crimes. Some of them had homosexual experience 'outside'; others had become homosexual, or given way to homosexual feelings for the first time, in the all-male environment in which they had been placed.

The homosexuality in prison, however, appeared – both at Winchester and at Wormwood Scrubs, where I was sent later – to be almost exclusively of the emotional kind. There was very little physical contact, because there were so few opportunities for it. What did happen – and I saw it happen again and again – was that two men became drawn together in a relationship so deep, happy, and lasting that it can only be described as love.

Two such men would take little trouble to disguise their relationship, because, in prison, no stigma attached to it. It was accepted – and this was something I had never known before – as a logical extension of the relationship between a working-class man and his 'mate'. It was, in fact, regarded by prisoners and warders alike as perfectly normal.

I have seen it suggested, in a recent book by two ex-convicts from Dartmoor, that for every homosexual who goes into gaol, two come out. This may be literally true, but not in the sense that men are introduced to homosexual practices in prison. A chance homosexual act, induced by the absence of women, does not make a man into a homosexual for the rest of his life. What may do so is a deep emotional attachment, such as I have described, with another man. The real danger in sending homosexuals to gaol lies in the fact that other prisoners may adopt their outlook, rather than their habits. As a punishment, it is strangely inappropriate. As a deterrent, it is worse than useless.

*

Edward Montagu, Michael Pitt-Rivers, and I remained together at Winchester for five weeks. This made the first shock of imprisonment much easier to bear; none of us had the feeling of total isolation which, in those first weeks, must be the worst punishment of most convicted men. We did not, however, compose ourselves into an exclusive group, although we had been warned by the authorities against making friends with other prisoners.

The Chaplain, an amiable and sympathetic man, told me later that when we arrived the other prisoners and the warders had been 'watching like hawks' for any false steps on our part, particularly on that of Lord Montagu. I remember the first day that we queued up for our mid-day meal, each carrying a plastic tray divided into compartments for soup, meat, and pudding.

'You see that little room what we just passed?' asked the mutineer, who was standing next to me in the queue. 'Know what it is?'

I said I imagined it was some kind of store-room, since it appeared to be full of wheelbarrows and sacks of flour.

'No, it's where the blokes drop down into after they've been topped. The condemned cell's on the landing just above. Cor, look at Monty getting his dinner!'

Edward was holding out his tray. The warder-cook ladled out soup, two slices of gristly meat, a wedge of washed-out cabbage and three potatoes. One of the potatoes rolled off the spoon. Edward picked it up off the table with his fingers and deposited it in his tray.

This incident caused as much of a consternation as if a General Amnesty had been declared. All the other prisoners nudged each other, pointed and beamed. After that, Edward was 'Monty' to everyone in the prison.

He was not, however, quite so popular with the Governor. Like me, he had started off on the wrong foot. At the 'Reception' interview he had been asked: 'What are you going to do when you are released?' and had replied that he was going to carry on exactly as before. He meant, of course, that he would continue to devote most of his time to the management of his estate at Beaulieu, but the reply was unfortunately phrased.

'If you do,' observed the Governor, his hackles rising, 'you will most certainly pay a return visit to this institution.'

We had become quite accustomed, by now, to being mis-understood by the prison 'higher-ups'. The ordinary warders, known to everybody as 'screws' and to each other as 'Officers', were on the whole much easier to talk to.

One of them asked Edward how he found prison life.

'Not much worse than the Guards Depot at Caterham, thank you.'

'Ah yes, I was in the Guards myself. And in a Jap POW camp after that.'

'It's wonderful what one can put up with, isn't it?'

'Well, it might have happened to anybody, you know. Most people have something in their private lives that wouldn't bear looking in to.'

Edward told me of this conversation, which we both thought rather odd. If either of us had been in a prisoner of war camp, the last career we would have taken up on our release was that of prison warder.

I asked one of the burglars why he thought anybody became a 'screw'. He said: 'Because they're too bloody idle to do anything else.'

There were no facilities for Association at Winchester, so we ate our meals in our cells. Association is a fairly new privilege which has now been introduced at most prisons containing first offenders. The men have their meals together, and afterwards are allowed to talk, listen to the wireless, play chess or draughts and read the newspapers. We missed the news-papers very much, but the other prisoners used to cut out any mention of our case and slip the cuttings into our pockets during exercise, with appropriate comments pencilled in the margin. This was, of course, strictly forbidden; and, looking back now on my time at Winchester, I seem to have spent most of it in tearing up pages of newsprint into fragments small enough to flush down the lavatory. The *Daily Sketch* had said:

The verdict is – Guilty. Lord Montagu of Beaulieu, Michael Pitt-Rivers and Peter Wildeblood are sentenced to terms of imprisonment. Yet doubt remains. . . .

Not concerning the trial itself. It was conducted with scrupulous fairness, and we have no doubt that on the evidence before them the jury came to an honest decision.

But there will be disquiet in the public mind at the way in which these three men were hunted down. The evidence against them hinged almost entirely on the testimony of self-confessed perverts, who were at least as guilty as the men in the dock.

There are plenty of precedents for the use of criminals to bring other criminals to justice. But why should these three men go to gaol while their two accomplices, who were described by counsel as of the 'lowest moral character', go free?

The sentences passed will undoubtedly revive the controversy whether imprisonment is a suitable punishment for such offences. But in this case arguments about the possibilities of psychiatric or medical treatment are pointless. The court had to deal with the law as it stands : and, on that basis, justice has been done.

If the law is a bad law, as psychiatrists and others contend, then it should be altered. There may be a good case for an investigation into the whole social problem of the control and punishment of perversion.

But that is for the future – and for Parliament to decide.

Hannen Swaffer wrote in the *People* :

The sentences in the Montagu Case have caused glee in ultra-respectable circles, consternation and fear among many celebrities in the world of the stage, art and letters, and exposed the complete failure of our so-called 'civilization' to find any remedy for sexual perversion to replace cruel and barbaric punishment. . . . Society must realize that imprisonment is no cure for abnormality. Shutting up a nervous, highly-strung individual is mere brutality that increases, instead of removing, a psychological weakness. . . . Montagu and his two associates may have earned our condemnation. But they are also entitled to pity. They should be treated by psychopaths, not isolated by warders.

I particularly liked the suggestion about psychopaths.

The *Sunday Times* headlined its leading article: 'Law and Hypocrisy.' It said:

One may well ask whether, in regard to acts between consenting male adults, the truth is not that the real offence is to be found out. Notorious inverts occupy eminent places, and few people of wide acquaintance would be prepared to say that they know no-one whom they could suspect of conduct which – if found out – would bring legal punishment and social disgrace. In all this matter, our society is riddled with hypocrisy.

The law, it would seem, is not in accord with a large mass of private opinion. That condition always brings evil in its train: contempt for law, inequity between one offender and another, the risk of corruption of the police. . . . The case for a reform of the law as to acts committed in private between adults is very strong. The case for authoritative inquiry into it is overwhelming. An interim report under the auspices of the Moral Welfare Council of the Church of England has recently given that case clear support.

Such acts must be clearly distinguished from public indecency, from prostitution and importuning, and above all from corruption of the young. One of the arguments for reconsideration of the present criminal law is that, until this is done, the public conscience will not contrast sharply enough those things which must needs be legally tolerated, and those which must be condemned and rooted out.

It is the problem of the young that chiefly needs the constructive attention of social reformers and the public. Homosexual inversion is not now regarded by most psychologists as inborn, save in the sense that the possibility of it may be latent in any child: it can often be started or stimulated at a formative age. Parents, schoolmasters, doctors, ministers of religion, and all who have to do with youth, ought to be far more aware of the facts and the dangers than they commonly are, and more alert to protect and help those in their care.

This is the most important lesson of all that the scandals of recent months should have taught us.

Mr John Gordon, in the *Sunday Express*:

A disquieting episode disclosed at the Montagu trial demands urgent consideration. A detective-sergeant admitted that on the morning Pitt-Rivers was arrested in the country, he entered Pitt-Rivers' flat in London and searched it, without permission and without a warrant.

Now, I have always assumed – in common with most people – that in Britain a policeman has no right to enter any citizen's house and examine his property without the authority of a search warrant issued by a magistrate. We have been encouraged to believe that to be the vital difference between a Police State and a democracy. Have we been deluding ourselves? Do policemen really have a right to enter a house and rummage without a search warrant?

If they do, it seems to me a most alarming development. One other piquant question: Is the RAF corporal still a corporal?

The *New Statesman and Nation* :

The methods of the police in getting their evidence will have shocked public opinion more than in any case since the affair of Irene Savidge in 1927 – and may even result, as that case did, in a Royal Commission on police powers and procedure. It is hard to decide which is more repugnant, to have the police breaking into private houses, without even a search warrant from a magistrate, and reading men's private letters in order to prosecute them for incidents in their sex life (which an increasing number of people and newspapers are coming to feel is no concern of the law) or to see that evidence supported by the 'confessions' of accomplices obtained by a promise of immunity. The whole wretched case, which has, of course, won far more public interest than its intrinsic importance warrants, may nevertheless have far-reaching consequences.

Mr Alastair Forbes, in the *Sunday Dispatch* :

What the Montesi case has been to the Italian Press, the Montagu Case has been to the British. But there the resemblance ends. Excess, rather than lack of zeal on the part of the police has caused widespread surprise and dismay. The methods chosen to secure these convictions can hardly be generally approved. The emphasis with which the judge stressed that he was dealing as leniently with the prisoners as it was possible for him to do will also have been widely noted.

Few people can have read unmoved Mr Wildeblood's attempt to explain the tribulations suffered, it is clear, by many members of the community, who have had bad luck in their glandular development and have received an uneven distribution of the cells, or what you will, required to make a 'normal' man with 'normal' instincts. . . .

Enough is now known of sex inversion and its victims for many 'normal' people to say: 'There, but for the grace of God, go I.'

*

The Prison Commissioners had decided that we should not be allowed to finish our sentences together. It was, in any case, impossible for us to remain at Winchester, because it was not a 'Star' (first offenders) prison. We were told that Montagu would be going to Wakefield in Yorkshire, Pitt-Rivers to Maidstone, and I to Wormwood Scrubs.

I said good-bye to the mutineer, the various burglars, the jewel thief, and the man who had given me my first twist of tobacco. The man who had been in Sing-Sing said: 'The Scrubs should be better than this, anyhow. I expect they're sending you there for treatment. If you go into the hospital, it'll be a piece of cake.'

On the night before we left, I was interviewed by the Governor again. He made himself very pleasant and expressed further concern about my religious beliefs. He was, it seemed, a Roman Catholic himself, but he suggested that I should consider the various religions and pick from each one what seemed best to me. This was precisely what I had said to him myself at our first meeting.

His last words were: 'And don't go imagining that the law is going to be changed, or anything like that. Because it won't.'

I learned later that, on that very day, Sir David Maxwell Fyfe had at last yielded to the demands of Sir Robert Boothby and the Church of England that an official inquiry into homosexuality should be set up.

*

The journey to London – we were all going to the Scrubs first, and the other two on to Wakefield and Maidstone – was made by motor-coach. We had changed back into our own clothes, which felt light and silky after the rough prison uniforms.

We each carried a bundle of belongings, consisting in my case of a few letters and a very small pot of Marmite which I had bought out of my wages – 10d a week – at the canteen at Winchester. Edward had some magazines, which we shared between us. This time we were handcuffed; Edward and Michael together, leaving one hand of each free, I with my right hand chained to my left.

I thought of myself in a detached kind of way. Here I was, riding through Farnham in a bright orange coach, turning over the pages of the *New Yorker* with manacled hands. I should never feel quite the same again about the *New Yorker*, or Farnham, or the spring, which had hung its catkins along the road which I was travelling. I was becoming a different person. I had believed all my life that every experience, no matter how disagreeable, could be made to enrich and illuminate; this would be the test.

The purpose, or at least the effect, of sentencing a man to prison is to strip him of everything he has – of the possessions, the habits, the attitudes of mind that go to make up a distinguishable human personality. He is reduced to a common denominator of blank nakedness, as defenceless as the white caddis grubs that I used to watch in the stream of my childhood. But the grubs, I remembered, defended themselves by building a ramshackle armour out of whatever they found in the mud. Bits of decaying wood and broken shell, pieces of water-weed and grains of sand, were cemented together by the naked worm which, one day, would transform itself into a winged creature and climb up a reed-stalk into the sun. I would do the same.

The coach turned in at the gateway of Wormwood Scrubs. It was a huge, extravagantly architected place of dingy brick and grubby stone, with Romanesque colonnades running riot in all directions. The forecourt facing the Chapel looked like one of the unsuccessful designs for New Delhi.

We were given lunch in the Reception building, sitting on wooden benches and eating fried fish, cabbage, potato, and pudding out of a single deep, circular tin, with a spoon. Afterwards I said good-bye to Montagu and Pitt-Rivers, and they were taken away.

I stripped and had a bath before changing into the usual grey clothes. Then I went and collected my sheets, my pillow-slip, razor, and book of rules for the guidance of Convicted Prisoners, Male. I was shown into a cell on the third floor of 'D' hall. It was exactly the same as the one at Winchester, except that the floor was of scrubbed wooden boards. I had become used to such surroundings by now. I merely noted that the windows were dirty, the chamber-pot reasonably clean, and the mattress, as usual, full of lumps. I asked the duty warder for a bucket of cold water and a brush, and began to scrub the floor.

Next morning I was visited in my cell by Mr Cockayne, the principal officer in charge of 'D' Hall. He was rather a small man with ginger hair, blue eyes and a strong sense of drama.

Without an audience, he was lost. Even when he was addressing one prisoner, he kept looking around as though he hoped that someone else was listening.

He flung open my door with a theatrical crash. I was on my knees, trying to sweep some breadcrumbs on to a jagged piece of tin which did duty as a dustpan.

'Wildeblood, isn't it?' he boisterously inquired.

I said that it was.

'Well, I'm glad to see you intend to keep your cell clean. Begin as you mean to go on, that's what I say.' He stepped back a pace, swept the landing with his eyes and raised his voice. 'We keep up a pretty good standard here. Most of the floors are fairly decent. I do my best ... and then what happens? Lying swine' – his voice rising to a shriek – 'lying swine go and write books saying the place is filthy.' He gave me a meaning look and marched away, jerking his head from side to side and tugging at the seat of his trousers.

I rather liked Mr Cockayne. He reduced some of the prisoners to nervous wrecks with his continual nagging, but he very seldom punished anybody. He always treated me as though I were a time-bomb that might go off at any moment; partly, perhaps, because he suspected that I might have 'influence', partly because he knew I was a writer. He used to draw me aside and say: 'You know, Wildeblood, I honestly do my best to keep the place clean, but what can you do? The dirt isn't in the cells, it's here ... and here ... and here!' and his arm swung round in a circle to indicate the leaking roof, the grimy walls, and the disgusting lavatories which were not his responsibility, but that of the Prison Commissioners. It must have been heartbreaking for a man so obsessed with cleanliness, as Cockayne was, to have to work in a prison which was being allowed, quite callously and deliberately, to fall to pieces.

For he really was obsessed. I have seen him go quite pale with rage at the sight of a speck of dirt invisible to the naked eye of anybody else, and when newly-sentenced prisoners arrived wearing 'Teddy Boy' haircuts he almost had a seizure. His whole life was spent in a battle against an encroaching tide of dirt, which he regarded as a personal enemy; when he addressed the assembled prisoners one got the impression of Queen Elizabeth – whom he rather resembled in looks – spurring on her troops at Tilbury to repel an Armada composed of soot, spent matches, and bits of fluff. But it was just as well that somebody at Wormwood Scrubs should be fighting this battle, in which Mr Cockayne's superiors appeared to have lost all interest long ago.

I was allocated to the Tailors' Shop, a large and sunny room in which about eighty men were working at electric sewing machines, machines for knitting socks and other mechanical devices. In contrast to the Mailbag Shop at Winchester, there was, here, a positive feeling of industriousness. This was due, I discovered later, to the fact that many of the men were paid at piece-work rates. A really good worker on the sock-machines could earn as much as 6/– a week.

I was placed in front of a treadle-operated sewing machine and given a piece of shirt-tail on which to practise. As usual, the air was buzzing with ventriloquial conversations.

'How you doing, Pete?' asked my neighbour, a dwarfish, bald Cockney whom I had not met before. It took me a moment or two to find out who was speaking, since the words seemed to be issuing from his ears.

'O.K., thanks. How long have you been in?'

'Five weeks. Had me first visit Saturday. The mother-in-law.' He rolled his eyes plaintively. 'Cor, what a woman. The size of her! They could hardly get her through the gate. Screw on duty tried to turn her back, said they was only three allowed in at one time. Honest, I ain't kidding. You should have seen her in the War, though. Jerries was always trying to shoot her up; thought she was a barridge balloon. Straight. We got her into the old Anderson shelter in 1939 and she had to stay put for six years. Knit, she used to. All day and all night. We got her a pair of crowbars and there she sat, making wire-netting. You had a visit yet?'

'No, not yet.'

'First one'll shake you a bit, I expect. You get what they call a box visit, sitting there with a piece of glass between you. That's just for the first time; the others you sits at a table and they lets you have a good kiss-up at the end. It's all right. Cor, you should have seen the mother-in-law behind that glass! Laugh? She looked like a bloody porpoise in a 'quarium.'

There was a sharp hiss from the man on my other side. The older prisoners, I had noticed, usually removed their false teeth while working. It was not only more comfortable, but made it easier for them to converse without attracting the notice of the warders.

'Do you smoke?'

'Well, yes, when I've got any.'

'I'll see you're all right.' It was a Yorkshire accent this time. 'I read all about your case, you see, and I'd like to do this if you don't mind. I've nearly done my time, but I know what it's like when you first come in. Do you like marmalade?'

'Yes, very much.'

'I'll get you some. You don't have to pay me back.'

'But marmalade costs the earth – a shilling, at least.'

'That's my worry, not yours.'

'Well, thanks, anyway.'

'You're welcome.'

'Hey! Cut the cackle!' A warder came loping towards us. We all began to pedal, furiously.

*

There were two sit-down lavatories in the shop and two stand-up ones, shared by eighty prisoners. If one allows a session of ten minutes per man per day, it will be seen that this does not work out. Fortunately, most of the prisoners were chronically constipated, because of the food. They used the lavatories for surreptitious smoking, but this did not take so long; a prison cigarette, known as a 'roll-up', is only slightly thicker than a matchstick. The prisoners carry their tobacco – strong black shag – in a tin in their pockets, and roll a cigarette between their fingers as often as the opportunity arises. The ensuing 'dog-ends' are unpicked, re-rolled and smoked again, becoming more nauseating with each resurrection. Occasionally a warder, smoking a Woodbine, lets fall a 'tailor-made dog-end' which is eagerly snapped up.

In order to go to the lavatory it was necessary to attract a warder's attention, shout 'Fall out, sir?' and wait for the permissive nod. The warders, so wide awake when one was talking illicitly, always seemed to become deaf and blind when I wanted to go to the recess. In my agitation I sometimes forgot where I was, and on several occasions other prisoners had to restrain me from snapping my fingers at the 'Screws' as though they were inattentive waiters.

I soon discovered, however, which warders were 'all right' and which were not. They varied greatly. Some did not permit any talking at all, while others allowed the chatter to rise in an ear-splitting crescendo above the noise of the machines. One, known as 'Boots' because of the unusual size of his feet, boasted that his ambition was to become known as 'the worst screw in the nick'. He was always shouting fiercely and putting people on Governor's Report, the equivalent to a charge in the army. He was about 24 years old and had pleasant features which he was always pulling into strange shapes, like someone impersonating Humphrey Bogart. I was rather afraid of 'Boots' at first, but after a few weeks I discovered his horrible secret, which was that actually he had an extremely kind heart. One of the saddest things about Wormwood Scrubs was the number of old men, in their sixties and seventies, who had been sent to prison for a first offence. 'Boots', so harsh and scornful towards the younger prisoners, always took these old men under his wing, chatting to them when they looked depressed and occasionally slipping a 'dog-end' or a sweet into their pockets.

*

The newspapers, in their dear old-fashioned way, always consider it newsworthy when 'Public School Man Goes to Gaol'. The truth, sad though it may be, is that quite large numbers of public school men find their way to gaol, usually for shady business deals of one kind or another. At Wormwood Scrubs I met two Old Etonians, two Salopians, and a Wykehamist; there were doubtless many more. The result was that the snatches of conversation which one overheard on the exercise yard possessed a charming diversity.

I had, unconsciously, become so accustomed 'outside' to judging people by their clothes that I was slightly unnerved to discover, when everyone was wearing the same uniform, how wrong snap-judgements could be.

These two men, for example, beefy, red-faced and brutal; obviously planning together some act of violence. Dockers, perhaps, or professional chuckers-out. They come towards me:

'Always stay at the Georges Cinq, myself. Used to keep a suite there, actually. Expense account, you know.'

'I still say you can't beat the dear old Crillon.'

And these two; a thin, wolfish-looking young man with receding hair and horn-rimmed glasses, and his companion a fat waddling baby of about forty with round blue eyes:

'It's a doddle, I tell you. Two grand's worth of tom, and the old brass what's got it is stone potty. You could creep that drum six-handed, with jelly and all, and she'd think it was mice.'

It was an animated scene. The younger prisoners walked rapidly in twos or threes around the outside of the yard, watched by a warder at each corner. The older men, who could not walk so fast, ambled up and down in the centre. One of the old men kept darting into the outer circle, trying to beg a 'dog-end' from someone. I had noticed him before, in the Tailors' Shop, where he sewed buttons on to trousers. He was sixty-five years old, and his name was Ted. He had a rebellious quiff of white hair and very watery blue eyes. He had received a sentence of two years, supposedly for stealing a perambulator. The burglars said there must have been a baby in it.

There were several different kinds of burglars. There were the rank amateurs or 'slags' who had stolen paltry sums and were contemptuously described by the rest as 'gas-meter bandits'. Then there were those who had specialized in 'tom' (tom-foolery is rhyming slang for jewellery) and had done most of their work in hotels. These had a tendency towards Oxford accents and glib talk about Jaguars and the South of France; part of their stock-in-trade had, of course, been to look as little like burglars as possible. Finally, there were the professional house-breakers and safe-blowers, an exclusive – one might almost say snobbish – group whose members had usually known each other 'outside'. They looked very much like plumbers or carpenters, and their attitude towards their craft was much the same.

Cosh-boys, or 'blaggers', were rather rare, presumably because most of them came into the category of Young Prisoners and were therefore housed in 'C' Hall. The men who had been convicted of robbery with violence were usually excitable amateurs, who were somewhat despised by the professional housebreakers. A few of them were obvious mental defectives. If there was one thing more distressing at Wormwood Scrubs than the number of prisoners who should have been in Old People's Homes, it was the number who should have been in mental hospitals. They were always causing trouble, abusing privileges and causing fights. One or two of them were epileptics, as well.

The routine at Wormwood Scrubs varied in many details from that at Winchester, but once I had got used to it I found that the monotony of the days and nights, instead of making the time drag, made it go faster. Whole weeks went by almost unnoticed. I could tell which day of the week it was because each day had some small detail in which it differed from the rest. On Mondays there was fish for lunch, and the prisoners changed their handkerchiefs and plate-cloths. On Tuesday, instead of making their beds in the regulation manner, they hung their blankets and sheets over the landing railings to air. Wednesday was the day for changing library books. Thursday was bath-day. Friday was the day on which we were paid, and made our purchases from the canteen. On Saturday we did no work in the afternoon, but had a longer period of exercise. And we went to Church on Sundays.

After four weeks at Wormwood Scrubs – that is to say, after I had been in prison for nine weeks altogether – I was allowed to come out on Association. I sat at a table with nine other men on the ground floor of 'D' Hall, and after meals we moved our chairs to the wall, trying to keep as far away as possible from the lavatories, which were in constant use. Some men played darts, chess or draughts, but most of us just sat and talked and smoked our 'roll-ups'.

I always sat with the same group. Some of its members were sent eventually to open camps, some were released and others took their place, but it remained basically the same. The chairman, so to speak, was John, a 36-year-old timber merchant from Sussex. He was serving a seven-year sentence for a homosexual offence with a boy of 16. The boy, after staying in his house for some weeks, had left with all the valuables that he could carry away. John went to the police, and was prosecuted on the basis of his own statement. He pleaded guilty, having been told that it would be better for him if he did not oblige the boy to give evidence. The parents of the boy (who was not charged) were among a number of local residents who had petitioned for the sentence to be reduced, but nothing had been done. Leave to appeal had been refused. John had already done two years of his sentence when I met him, and his hair had gone quite grey. He looked about fifty. In spite of his own troubles, he always had time to listen to those of other people.

His particular friend was Jimmy, a young professional burglar who, like many of them, had been a Borstal boy. Jimmy was always talking about 'going straight', but it was hard to imagine that he ever would. He was too fond of American cars, flashy suits and the good things of life ever to settle down to a respectable, underpaid job. Sometimes, when he was depressed, he would make the resolution, knowing that he was due for a long spell of preventive detention next time: 'I ain't going to have no more of this.' Five minutes later he would be talking excitedly of forty-guinea suits, Pontiacs and '22-carat doddles', or crimes that couldn't go wrong. Somewhere in Jimmy's brain there was a large gap, where the sense of right and wrong should have been. His tragedy was that during all the time he had spent in Borstal and in prison, nobody had tried to supply this lack. He was extremely intelligent and quick, with a lively wit and a strong sense of honour towards his friends, but he was quite incapable of seeing that it was wrong to steal. At 22, there seemed to be nothing before him but a series of prison sentences, interrupted by bursts of wild spending.

Then there was Basil, the Wykehamist blackmailer. He was immensely tall, and spoke in a high-pitched scream. I had known him slightly at Oxford and he attached himself to me as soon as he arrived, to the discomfort of the burglars, who had never met anyone quite like him before. He used to make outrageous remarks about them in French, which they rightly resented. He was, however, such an amusing raconteur that they eventually accepted him, with reservations. He was undoubtedly one of the wickedest people I have ever met, but laughter is such a precious gift in prison that I was always glad when Basil came stalking towards me like a huge, bespectacled crane.

Vic was a river-pilot, who had been unable to resist the sight of an unattended barge containing some thousands of pounds' worth of copper ingots. One of his ancestors had been hanged for piracy in Execution Dock during the 17th century; Vic got four years. He was a tall, athletic young man with the most insatiable intellectual curiosity I have ever met. Since ships were his business, he had steeped himself in Conrad and Melville and Hakluyt and Darwin, and could talk about the sea for hours in a way that would have made Rachel Carson seem a landlubber. He had left school at 16 and had been educating himself ever since. Unlike most of the other men in prison, he was never bored for a moment. The only thing that worried him was his separation from his pretty young wife, always referred to as 'my Shirley Rose', and his baby son. They lived in a flat on top of a warehouse in Stepney, with the Thames outside the window. Shirley Rose kept rabbits in a garden on the roof, and it was Vic's ambition to build a dinghy up there and launch it over the side.

Charlie had been convicted of robbery with violence. He never discussed his crime, and we did not inquire. He was extremely thin, with hollow cheeks and a bony forehead, surmounted by an Edwardian quiff. Even in his prison uniform, Charlie was unmistakably a 'Teddy boy'. Although all the uniforms were supposed to be the same, Charlie's jacket seemed tighter than the rest, his lapels higher, the legs of his trousers narrower. I do not know whether he had surreptitiously altered them, or whether, by some occult means, his clothes had moulded themselves to his personality of their own accord. He was quiet and intensely shy, breaking out occasionally into a mad Chaplinesque performance as he described, with a brilliant sense of timing and satire, some event in his Camberwell past.

Another person with a shell of quietness and reserve was Bob, the research scientist. He had occupied a highly important post on a national Board, and had a wife and two daughters. His whole world had collapsed when he was found guilty of the fraudulent conversion of some trifling sum, and sentenced to three years in gaol. Gradually, however, we coaxed him out of his corner. We discovered that he had been in the Navy during the war, and Vic began talking to him about various ports they had both visited. He spoke very quietly, and every now and then his voice died away in the middle of a sentence. His eyes had that frightening, unfocused look that one often sees in prisoners. But one day Charlie started some ludicrous, fantastic pantomime, all scarecrow arms and legs and staccato Cockney patter, and Bob threw back his head and laughed. After that he was all right.

And then there was Dan Starling.

*

I noticed him first on the exercise yard, where he was talking to the birds. Wormwood Scrubs was inhabited by a large flock of pigeons, which were sustained by the bread put out by the prisoners on their window-ledges. In addition, at this time of year, there were numerous families of sparrows nesting in the eaves.

One of the fledgling sparrows had fallen out of its nest and lay, piping feebly, a few yards from the line of marching men. Dan picked it up and addressed the mother, who was looking out of a hole in the wall with her head cocked on one side.

'Hey, you!' he said, 'look after your own, can't you? Want the poor little bastard to get squashed?' He sounded quite angry. The fledgling lay in his big, calloused hands, opening and shutting its yellow beak.

'How about putting it on top of that pile of bricks?' I suggested. 'It doesn't look as if it can fly, but at least the mother can come down and feed it.'

'Yes, that's an idea. Hope the cats don't get it.' Dan reached up and put the bird on top of the bricks. He was about my own age, with a finely modelled, tanned face and fair hair brushed back from a high forehead. We walked on together.

'You're in the Tailors' Shop, aren't you?' he asked. 'I seen you when you come in. One thing, you don't look as bad as your picture in the papers.'

'Thanks.'

'Looked like you was dead or something. How's your bird going?'

'Bird?'

'Your porridge; your sentence.'

'Oh, quite quickly, really. I'll be out in March . . . only forty weeks more. How long are you doing?'

'Four and a half. I've done eighteen months, so I'm just half way.'

'Do you live in London?'

'I don't sound like it much, do I.' He grinned. 'Where did you think I come from?'

'Well, I – I hope you don't mind me saying so, but you look a bit like a gipsy.'

'Pretty shrewd, you are. My family's all Pikeys, but we ain't on the road no more. We lives in Hoxton.'

A voice bellowed: 'Form up!' It was time to go back to work.

'I'll be seeing you,' said Dan.

*

While I was still 'banged up' in my cell – that is, during my first month at the Scrubs – other prisoners had gone to a great deal of trouble to keep me abreast of the news. They used to copy out any relevant articles from the papers, in pencil, on lengths of toilet paper, and hand them to me, rolled up, when no-one was looking. In this way I learned that *The Times* had published two long and authoritative articles on 'Homosexual Offenders', expressing the view that the laws under which I had been prosecuted should be abolished; and that the same view had been put forward by the *Observer*. Reynolds and McNally had been dismissed from the RAF, and Sir David Maxwell Fyfe sharply questioned in the House of Commons about the illegal searches carried out by the police. His answers, evasive and misleading, drew the following comment from a reader of the *Sunday Express* :

I am disappointed in Sir David Maxwell Fyfe. As Home Secretary he should act as a guardian of the people's liberties. Instead, he seems far too ready to sacrifice individual freedom to police convenience.

I cite his extraordinary statement to the House of Commons over the police search of Major Pitt-Rivers' London flat, made without a warrant after the arrest of Pitt-Rivers in Dorset.

Sir David said that the search was carried out with the consent of the person (a Mr Anderson) to whom the key of the flat had been entrusted.

But in evidence at Lymington, the police officer concerned stated:

'1. He had advised Mr Anderson not to get in touch with Mrs Pitt-Rivers. (Why?)
'2. That Major Pitt-Rivers had been arrested on a warrant for a felony. (*This was false.*)
'3. That Mr Anderson objected to letting the police in. ("Consent"?)'

Sir David also said it has long been the practice that when the police arrest a person on private premises, a search is carried out on those premises.

But has it really been the practice for the police to search every other possible home of the arrested man, in his absence, and without a warrant? If so, the practice should be changed.

Sir David should realize this; to uphold the great principles of English justice is far more important than any individual's suspected misdemeanours.

We don't want even a suspicion of the practices of a police State here.

Ministerial lying on the grand scale was not, however, the only activity that had been taking place at Westminster. The House of Lords had been debating a motion 'calling attention to the incidence of homosexual crime in Britain', set down by Earl Winterton.

Lord Winterton had been, for many years, the Conservative MP for the district in which my parents lived. During my trial, my mother had written to him, asking him, whatever the verdict might be, to take up with the Home Secretary the various questions of police behaviour which had been raised by the case. Lord Winterton replied that he had every sympathy with her personally, but that he was unable to do anything as he no longer sat in the Commons, and that anyhow provincial police forces did not come under the control of the Home Secretary. Having got this off his chest, he went to the House of Lords and said:

In some circles that ought to know better, there has been a whispering campaign against the police for the action they have taken. I believe that to be entirely unjustified. The police have been fully justified in all the action they have taken in recent cases.

He attacked the Church of England for its criticisms of the law, and, as *The Times* put it, 'blurted out' the name of a well-known actor who had recently been fined for importuning.

'Many of the great actors of the past, in the early days of the century,' he said, 'were my friends. It was inconceivable that they would have been guilty of the disgusting offence of male importuning. . . . I am convinced that the majority of the British people agree that nothing lowers the prestige, weakens the moral fibre, and injures the physique of a nation more than tolerated and widespread homosexuality.'

His speech also included the phrases 'filthy, disgusting and unnatural vice' and 'corrosive and corrupting immorality'.

Lord Jowitt, following this with a calm and reasonable speech, said that when he had been Attorney-General 95 per cent of all blackmail cases had a homosexual origin. We must not make the mistake of trying to make our criminal law cover the same ground as the moral law: adultery was a great evil, but no-one would suggest that it should once more be made a criminal offence. He congratulated the Government on their courage in setting up a Committee to investigate the law.

Lord Vansittart and Lord Ammon supported Lord Winterton. Lord Chorley said that he regretted their 'emotional' approach. Lord Ritchie of Dundee said that as far as the private actions of adults were concerned, he believed that public opinion generally would be glad to see an end to prosecutions.

Lord Brabazon of Tara said that 'a recent case' had had curious repercussions. That the police should question one of two guilty men for more than 10 hours in order to get him to turn Queen's Evidence, and promise him immunity in order to convict the other, might be all right in foreign countries, but was very much against public approval here. The result was that, instead of public condemnation going against the condemned, it had gone against the police for their methods. That had been a very shocking and terrible thing. 'If the law is such as to encourage over-zealous police departments to indulge in those sorts of methods,' declared Lord Brabazon, 'it is time for the law to be changed.'

The Times headlined its report of the debate: 'PEERS ENDORSE INQUIRY INTO HOMOSEXUALITY. POWER OF PUBLIC OPINION.' The *Daily Mail*, it may be noted, curtailed all the speeches except that of Lord Winterton, which it reported in full under the headline: 'SEX VICE: VETERAN PEER SPEAKS OUT' – a fair example of the *Daily Mail* technique of telling its readers rather less than half the truth.

Mr John Gordon, whose column 'Current Events' enlivens the *Sunday Express*, added his voice to that of Lord Winterton.

'An emotional crusade,' he wrote, 'seems to be developing to legalize perversion, and even to sanctify perverts . . . STUFF AND NONSENSE. Perversion is very largely a practice of the too idle and the too rich. It does not flourish in lands where men work hard and brows sweat with honest labour.

'It is a wicked mischief, destructive not only of men but of nations. Those who are raising sentimental howls in its defence would do Britain a better service by lending their support to stamping it out.'

When I read this tirade, carefully copied out on toilet-paper, I laughed as I had not done for months. 'The idle rich'? When convicted homosexuals include seven times as many factory workers, and twice as many farm labourers, as men of independent means? 'Lands where men work hard'? What about the Scandinavian countries, Belgium, Holland, Switzerland, and Germany, in none of which it is considered necessary to carry out periodic witch-hunts against homosexual scapegoats?

As for 'emotional crusades' and 'sentimental howls', it was pretty obvious which side in this controversy was being most emotional, and howling the loudest. The posturings of Lord

Winterton were the most ludicrous of all, with his claim that none of his friends had been homosexuals, because for years he had been a close friend of Lawrence of Arabia.

It was not until many months later, however, that I discovered the full extent of Lord Winterton's hypocrisy. During the second reading of the Criminal Justice Bill on November 27th, 1947, he had drawn attention to the fact that the bill contained no reference to homosexual crime.

I think his words on that occasion are worth repeating. He said: 'I would draw attention to two gross anomalies. One is the very inadequate penalties for cruelty to children. The other is that the penalty for unnatural vice between male persons is too high. Only comparatively recently, I understand, has that been a crime under English Law. I think that the present penalty was largely introduced as a result of the obstructions on another Bill by Mr Henry Labouchere. I understand that there is no penalty for Lesbianism. . . . '

*

One morning I looked out of my cell door – I had been moved to the fourth floor by now – and saw, standing on the landing below, a man whose face was vaguely familiar. Was he someone I had known in Fleet Street? Or in the RAF, or perhaps at school? Then I realized who he was. The man, standing there in prisoner's uniform, was the warder who had said to Edward Montagu during our first days at Winchester: 'It might happen to anybody.' It had happened to him.

Later, on exercise, I found him walking alone. I gave him two 'roll-ups' and a matchstick split in four, for which he was just as grateful as I had been on my first day in prison. He told me that he had been convicted of carnal knowledge of his own daughter aged twelve. The judge at Winchester had expressed sympathy with him, and sentenced him to three years' imprisonment. On the day after he arrived at the Scrubs, the Governor made him a 'Red Band' – that is to say, gave him privileges which other prisoners had to wait months or even years to acquire.

This news enraged Charlie, Vic, Jimmy, and Dan, who, rightly or wrongly, believed that the man had been given this post in return for a promise to inform on any other prisoners who were breaking regulations. It enraged me, too, when I contrasted his treatment with that of Ron.

Ron was a 22-year-old farm labourer from a small village in Sussex. He had committed sexual offences with several small boys, had been found out, and was persuaded by the police, in the usual way, to plead guilty. He was quite stupid and was, in fact, described in court by the police as having a mental age of 12. During the questioning, he told the police that he had been seduced, when he was himself a small boy, by a gardener who was still living in the village. The gardener was also arrested, and he, too, pleaded Guilty. They both came up before the same judge for sentence, at Lewes Assizes.

Judges frequently justify savage sentences by telling the convicted man that his crime has ruined a human life, by causing his victim to become a homosexual for the rest of his days. I do not think this theory is true, but it is one which judges employ. The judge in this case apparently took this view, because he sentenced the gardener to seven years' imprisonment.

He then turned to Ron. One might have expected some leniency for the victim, for this illiterate farm-boy with a mental age of 12, whose parents had promised to try to help him and whose employer had agreed to take him back. The judge gave him five years.

As so often happens, Ron and the gardener were both sent to Wormwood Scrubs. When I last saw them they had been there for a year, seeing each other almost every day. Neither of them had been offered any help during that time by psychiatrist or doctor. One day, an Assistant Governor, a man who professed to be a Christian, visited Ron in his cell.

'Well,' he asked, 'have you made up your mind to change your habits when you get outside?'

'How can I?' said Ron. 'Every day I see the man who started it all. I keep on remembering. Sir, can't I be sent somewhere else, so that I can get away from him?'

The Assistant Governor smiled. 'That's all part of the punishment,' he said.

*

The arrival of summer was signalled by a blaze of purple irises which bordered the exercise yard. The prisoners in 'C' Hall were allowed to pick them and place them in polished Harpic tins on their dining-tables, but 'D' Hall, under the austere and hygienic eye of Mr Cockayne, remained undecorated. On sunny days the heat in the Tailors' Shop was overpowering; the windows could only be opened by lifting them bodily out of their frames, and we were still wearing the same clothes, grey flannel, thick woollen socks and heavy shoes. Every evening, by the time I returned to my cell, I was coated with a sticky mixture of sweat, dust, and cinders. I used to strip and stand in my metal wash-basin, sponging myself with a rag soaked in cold water and trying not to dirty my scrubbed floor.

Every Thursday morning we were marched off to the Bath House, a one-story building divided into cubicles and containing about thirty bath-tubs. The water was copious and hot, and the 'screw' in charge did not hurry us unduly. Bath-day was therefore an event to look forward to. For some reason there were no plugs in the baths and the first thing we had to do was to find a piece of shirt-tail, wring it out in Dettol – the only disinfectant, incidentally, in the prison was this tin of Dettol in the bath-house – and stuff it into the plug-hole. Then we took off our clothes, wrapped a towel round us and went to collect a clean shirt, underwear, and socks from a store-room supervised by a prisoner. There was always a good deal of argument about this, because the shirts were invariably un-ironed and often had large holes in them, like the socks, while the underwear was of the most eccentric shapes and was usually devoid of buttons.

It was a lordly experience, to sink into a deep, hot bath and watch the prison dirt detach itself from one's body and form a grey, scurfy line along the sides of the tub. The tablets of soap with which we were provided had been manufactured, I think, from boiled-down fragments and had a peculiar, limp consistency, but Dan Starling, whose earnings amounted to five shillings a week, used to present me from time to time with a tablet of Lux toilet soap from the canteen. I had never noticed before that Lux soap had such a powerful perfume; in contrast,

I suppose, to the usual prison smells it seemed as pungent as a bowl of hyacinths.

Since the weekly bath was our only source of hot water, most of us washed our hair in it, emerging in a golliwog-like condition of which Mr Cockayne could hardly be expected to approve. The problem of hair-oil was acute, and we solved it in three ways. Some of us, if we were sufficiently well-paid, would save up for weeks in order to buy a bottle of Vaseline Hair Tonic, which cost half a crown. Others would use melted margarine, or skim off the cocoa-butter which floated greasily on their evening mug of cocoa. The third stratagem was to bribe one of the prisoners who acted as servers in the Roman Catholic church to steal the oil out of the votive lamp; it was said to be pure olive oil and was highly prized.

On Thursdays, for a few hours, we were as clean as kings; for the rest of the week we stayed dirty. There were two wash-basins in the Shop in which, officially, we were supposed to wash our hands before going to meals. These were provided with cold water, and no soap or towels; furthermore, their use was effectively prevented by the rule that only two men were allowed in the recess at the same time. Men who had been working all morning amid dust and grease, and who had probably visited the lavatory as well, therefore went off with un-washed hands to lunch, to break their bread and mop up the soup, and afterwards to wash up the dishes in lukewarm water with no soap or detergent. Among the prisoners I knew there was at least one who was receiving treatment for syphilis.

According to the book of rules for the guidance of Convicted Prisoners the chamber-pots in our cells were intended for the purpose of making water during the night. As we were locked up in our cells for fourteen hours every day they were, of course, used for defecation as well. We emptied them out every morning and rinsed them in cold water. There was no disinfectant, but about once every three months we were given a tablespoonful of Harpic. By this time the pots were usually lined with an evil-smelling crust of dried urine.

The lavatories on the landing – one to every 22 cells – were frequently blocked up. After I had been at Wormwood Scrubs for several months I thought it might be interesting to see what happened if I complained about this. In theory, every prisoner had the right to see the Governor if he had a complaint to make. The procedure was as follows:

I had to get up as soon as the bell was rung at 6.30 a.m., make up the bed, tidy my cell, wash and get my face lathered ready for the razor. When the warder came round with the blade I had to shave hurriedly, rush with my chamber-pot to the recess, empty it, rinse out my wash-basin and fetch more cold water for the evening, finish dressing and find the warder in charge of the landing, to give him back my razor-blade and get permission to make a Governor's Application. This was officially supposed to be done before 7 o'clock and, as the blades were often not issued till 7.10 there was always the chance of being told that it was too late.

In theory, it was only necessary to apply to the Landing Officer before seeing the Governor. In practice, Mr Cockayne insisted on seeing every prisoner who made an Application, so that he could find out what they were complaining about. I therefore had to go down to the ground floor and stand in a queue outside Mr Cockayne's office. The man in front of me was a character called Dizzy, who often talked to himself and had been known, on occasion, to start screaming, quite suddenly. He glared at me suspiciously and mumbled something about mice.

I followed Dizzy into the office. Mr Cockayne smiled amiably and, cocking his head towards Dizzy, remarked: 'Scruffy-looking type, isn't he? What can you do with men like that?'

I said that you could always put them into lunatic asylums, since Dizzy was in my opinion not so much scruffy as potty.

'Ah!' said Mr Cockayne, 'I quite agree, but that's a problem for the medicos. All I can do is to try and keep them clean. Now, what can I do for you?'

I said that the lavatory on the North End side of the fourth landing had been blocked up for several days, and was beginning to smell. The pan had overflowed, and the contents were forming a pool on the floor.

'People *will* throw chunks of bread down them,' said Mr

Cockayne crossly. 'They've got no imagination. Is it next to your cell?'

I said that, fortunately, it was not.

'Well, I'll tell the Works about it.'

The Works was a depressed-looking party of prisoners who went round poking in the plumbing with a flexible rod known as a Snake.

'Thank you, sir.'

'You're getting on all right, are you? Not having too bad a time?'

'Not too bad, sir.'

'That's good. I'm glad you've made up your mind to do your sentence the easy way. We get some men who spend all their time complaining, you know. The other prisoners put them up to it.'

'I hope you don't think anybody's put me up to this, sir. I just thought you ought to know.'

'O.K., but you want to be careful, you see. There's a lot of villains in here.' This was a standing joke, at which we both laughed in a ritualistic manner. 'I don't like to see people like yourself mixed up with a lot of hooligans, it doesn't seem right.'

I went away. The lavatory remained blocked, standing defiantly in the middle of a brownish lake. I complained to the Landing Officer, to the officer in charge of Works, and to Mr Cockayne again. It remained blocked for six weeks. Eventually the Snake was inserted to unheard-of depths, and emerged with a dented Golden Syrup tin. 'There,' said Mr Cockayne, 'what did I tell you? Hooligans.'

*

When a man arrives in gaol, he is warned against becoming too friendly with the other prisoners. This may be good advice, but it is not very practical. Prison is a forcing-house for friendships, desirable or otherwise; it would be quite impossible to spend one's whole sentence in self-imposed solitary confinement.

The two warder-instructors in the Tailors' Shop, who

eventually became good friends of mine, were always warning me, at the beginning, against Dan.

'I see you're walking round with that Starling. I wouldn't, if I were you. He's no good.'

'How do you know?' I asked.

'I know all right. I've seen too many of them. Approved School, Borstal, the Scrubs, and then a nice long spell at Wandsworth or the Moor. If he was ever going to go straight he'd have done it long ago.'

'Nobody seems to be doing much to change his mind, do they?'

'What's the use? You can't do anything with blokes like that. They've got to make up their own minds, that's all. Starling's always fiddling something.'

I knew that this was true. During the last few weeks Dan had 'fiddled' a number of things, usually for my benefit. They included two raw onions, which I had eaten secretly in the middle of the night, and an orange, which had caused endless trouble. Fruit of any kind was entirely unknown at the Scrubs, and I was haunted for days afterwards by pips and fragments of peel, which shot mysteriously out of my clothing whenever I was speaking to a warder.

'Dan,' I asked, when we were next on exercise together, 'what are you going to do when you finish this lot?'

'Go screwing again, I suppose.' Screwing meant burglary. 'Why?'

'Well, there ain't nothing else I can do, is there? Got to earn a living somehow.'

'And get pinched again, and do eight years' P.D.?'

'Sounds bad to you, doesn't it?'

'I think it's a pity. Dan, how did all this begin?'

He told me the story. His father was a hopeless drunk: 'He's been through the whole bloody lot, and now he's on the Hilda Glider – that's cider – and when they get on that you can't do nothing with them. He pushes one of them handcarts round, delivering bread, and most nights he just crawls into the barrow and goes to sleep among the loafs.' Dan's mother was living with another man. She had had a great struggle to bring up the family, and the children spent most of their time hanging around on the streets and playing on bomb-sites. At eleven, Dan had got into trouble with the police. He and a gang of other small boys had been found at the Zoo, trying to break open a slot machine to get at the chocolate. I forget the exact details of Dan's progress as a juvenile delinquent, but it all began with the slot machine. Instead of being given 'a clip over the earhole' by his father, he was brought in front of a juvenile court and, from then on, was technically a person with a 'record'.

At sixteen, he went to Borstal. 'I didn't know nothing when I went in,' he said, 'but by the time I come out I was as shrewd as any of them.' From the older boys he picked up all the tricks of the burglar's trade, and learned to look upon himself as a man at war with Authority. He went into the Army and was moved from regiment to regiment before eventually being discharged with ignominy. After the war he worked for a gang of safebreakers, until he was caught. It was a terrible story, and one that seemed to give no grounds for hope.

But who was I to judge? I was, after all, a criminal myself. It was no use complaining that I was misunderstood by Society, if I made no attempt to understand people like Dan. I did not believe there was anything I could do, but I passionately wanted to know – how had all this come about? Was it inevitable? And whose fault was it? Had Dan chosen to be the sort of person he was, or had the choice been made for him?

'How much tobacco have you got in your tin?' I asked.

'Half an ounce. Why?'

'If somebody pinched a quarter you'd yell blue murder, wouldn't you?'

'Not half. I'd kick his teeth in.'

'Well, if you feel that way, can't you see how people feel when their houses get burgled?'

''Tisn't the same,' said Dan.

'Why not?'

'Well, for one thing, the people as gets burgled is usually insured; for a damn sight more than the stuff is worth, like as not. I bet half of them is glad to see the last of it. I mean to say, supposing some geezer has given a couple of grand's worth of diamonds to some bird, and then maybe he gets sick of her – wouldn't he rather have the insurance money?'

'Yes, possibly, but what about all the people who are under-insured, or not insured at all?'

'That's their look-out, isn't it? Anyhow, I think screwing private houses is a mug's game, unless you know there's something worth having. Office safes is the best line. There's always someone in a place like that what'll go bent, if you promise him a big enough cut.'

'What, a night watchman or someone?'

'Yes, usually. You have to tie them up, of course, and sometimes bash them about a bit, just to make it look like they're not on the firm. Not so as to hurt, naturally.'

This Robin Hood view of things seemed a little too good to be true. 'What about all the robbery-with-violence cases one hears about, then?' I asked.

'Well, there's two kinds of R.W.V., Pete. There's the silly slags what goes around coshing people regardless because it's the only way they know to make a tickle. Then there's the professionals what gets charged with robbery-with-violence just to make it stick better – which is quite a different matter. For instance, suppose there's some screwsman that the law's got an eye on; they can't pin nothing on him but they think he should go inside for a nice long time, if it can be arranged. For the sake of argument, let's say he's got a little tickle planned at a private house, and somebody grasses on him. If they nick him for screwing, pure and simple, it'll probably be two years or maybe three, so what do they do?'

'They can't very well charge him with robbery-with-violence unless somebody's been hurt,' I said.

'Oh, that's all cobblers. If it's a tie-up, arranged beforehand, they can usually get the person to say they've been coshed as well.'

'How?'

'By promising not to charge them as an accomplice, of course. Blimey, do I have to tell *you*? What about McNally, for Christ's sake?'

'Yes, but doesn't there have to be a weapon?'

'There always is. I've known blokes be charged with

"armed robbery" because they had steel tips to their heels. Or because they was carrying a packing-case opener. I tell you, you can't win. The law's got it on you, every time.'

That night after tea – a hunk of bread, a pat of margarine, and a spoonful of watered jam – Basil came and sat next to me. He and Bob were working in the Library, the staff of which, apart from them, consisted exclusively of confidence-men of the most boring kind, who spent most of their time in trying to impress each other with their social qualifications. There was one whom Basil particularly detested. His name was Glubb, and he had formerly been a Councillor for one of the London boroughs.

'What sort of a day have you had, and how was Councillor Glubb?' I asked.

'My God, I wish you'd been there,' said Basil. 'Bob and I have been sorting out the Theological section. It's full of the most peculiar old tracts and Mormon hymn-books and things. There's one shelf that really made us laugh most frightfully, though; it's labelled "French, Devotional" and can you guess what the first volume is? Of all things, the memoirs of the Duc de St Simon! I pointed it out to Bob and of course we both *died*, and that ghastly old nightmare Glubb looked over the top of his spectacles at us and said: "*Some* people seem to think they come to prison in order to *laugh*." It was too much, really. What have you been doing?'

'Actually, trying to find out what makes burglars tick. Dan Starling, in particular.'

'Very dangerous, I should think, but probably quite entertaining as well. All the usual glib rationalizations, I suppose?'

'In a way, yes, but I think he believes them himself.'

'Oh, probably. I will say this for your Starling, you know: when I came in here I looked around and I thought – "All these people are dead." You know what I mean, don't you? That funny look in the eyes, and not seeming to listen when one's talking. Well, I looked at Dan and I thought, goodness, here's somebody who's still alive. I don't know how he manages it, after nearly two years.'

I looked at Dan. Yes, he was alive.

'And another thing, he's really most terrifically kind. To

you, I mean; not to anyone else. I've been trying for weeks to get him to buy me some sweets, but he won't, he's far too busy looking after you. There's a lot of good in him really, but heaven knows what'll happen when he gets out of here. Back to the old life of crime, I suppose. Bunny, for God's sake stop throwing yourself about, I don't want to be your next victim.'

Bunny was a film cameraman of remarkably spindly physique, with horn-rimmed glasses and an excitable manner, who had been convicted of causing Grievous Bodily Harm to his wife. He was a rather timid creature, and none of us could understand how he could have caused Grievous Bodily Harm to anyone, except possibly by his expansive gestures; he was incapable of talking without throwing his arms and legs about in an agitated manner which, as Basil pointed out, might be excessively dangerous in a confined space.

'I'm very, very cross,' said Bunny, waving like a windmill. 'Vic's making uncalled-for remarks about my private life.'

Vic leaned back in his chair, crossed his legs and grinned spaciously. 'I was only asking where his old woman was now,' he explained.

'You know perfectly well that she's trying to divorce me,' said Bunny. 'I went on Governor's Application this morning to get a special letter to my solicitor. I think it's most unfair of her.'

'What's she divorcing you for?' asked Bob.

'Hitting her over the head with an umbrella,' suggested Basil, 'the big brute.'

'Nothing of the sort. Something much worse.'

'Oo, go on, tell us,' pleaded Vic.

'Well, I don't really know what it means.'

'Come on, Bunny, don't be shy.'

'It's too embarrassing.'

'Bunny, I shall hit you.'

'Moral degeneracy, whatever that is,' said Bunny, blushing.

Vic slapped his knees and hooted with laughter. '*I* know,' he said. 'You been pissing in the sink.'

*

I was still working in the Tailors' Shop, but had by now been transferred to one of the machines for making button-holes. There were two of these, and they were said to have been constructed in 1890. Mine was called Potemkin, and the other Alice; the names had been scratched on their enamelled bases by some long-released prisoner. Alice was operated by an Australian adventurer who had incurred the displeasure of the police by owning five passports more than he was entitled to. We used to talk to each other, for no sensible reason, in squeaky pidgin-English, varying the routine occasionally by pretending to be Japanese prisoners with no roofs to our mouths. I do not know how this fantasy arose, but by the time Bill was posted to an open camp we had composed an entire parody of 'Oklahoma!' in roofless Japanese, called 'Yokohama!'

The machines, when they were in the mood, were capable of making a buttonhole in one-and-a-half minutes, but they were always going wrong. This was a considerable source of annoyance to the prisoners who were making trousers on piece-work rates. Some of them thought we were doing it on purpose.

There was one Jewish prisoner who suspected us profoundly. He would come bustling up to our table, inquiring plaintively: 'What have you done with my flies?'

'We've broken down,' said Bill. 'Come back on Tuesday week.'

'Yes, it's all very well, but it affects my pay, you know. Can't you possibly get on a little quicker?'

'Finkelstein, you're a one-man sweatshop,' said Bill. 'What's a few pennies, more or less?' and he dived under the machine, softly humming one of our songs, 'The Sulley with the Flinge on Top.'

'Supposing,' said Mr Finkelstein, leaning forward in a conspiratorial manner, 'supposing I gave each of you a Woodbine?'

This was bribery on the grand scale. I got out my tobacco-tin and pushed it carelessly under a pile of trouser-flies. 'Tell me, Mr Finkelstein,' I said, 'why are you so rich? I saw you coming out of the canteen last week with a pot of marmalade *and* a bag of biscuits.'

'Ah, you see, I have a system. Every week I put away a little something, and in that way one creates a small reserve.' He pulled two slightly battered Woodbines out of his overall pocket and slid them into my tin. As he waddled away, Bill sighed. 'Marvellous, isn't it?' he said. 'That bloke treats his two bob a week just like it was two hundred quid.'

This was a feature of prison life which I had often noticed. Since tobacco was the common currency, the attitude of each prisoner towards it provided a faithful reflection of the attitude to money which he had had 'outside'. The miser hoarded his 'snout' as carefully as though it were a bag of gold; the cadger devoted all his ingenuity to borrowing other people's fag-ends; the spendthrift smoked like a chimney all through the week-end, and then went without until Friday; the financial wizard created a commercial empire based on a capital of two ounces and an interest-rate of 50% per week. Men fought over a cigarette as they would have done over buried treasure. They sold their food for 'roll-ups' and used them to bribe prisoners in privileged positions: a clean shirt cost two cigarettes, a pot of Marmite stolen from the hospital a quarter of an ounce.

There were two further subjects which occupied men's minds. One was the possibility of escape; the other, that of being posted from Wormwood Scrubs to another prison.

There were many among us who were condemned to spend another three, five or seven years in gaol, but I never found one who could accept the fact in the sense of settling down to a permanent, monotonous routine which would not vary during the next thousand or two thousand days. They simply refused to believe that in, say, 1960 they would still be sitting in this dark, smelly place, still watching the dart-players and wondering whether their cell-floor were clean enough to pass muster. When I first went to the Scrubs there was some hope for these men, because the policy of the Prison Commissioners appeared to be to move long-sentence prisoners to Wakefield after they had done eighteen months of their sentence. Listening to them talking about Wakefield, one would have imagined that they were discussing Paradise. There would be no more chivvying about; there was talking and even music in the workshops; the cells were left open until 8.45 p.m. so that the

142

prisoners had a choice of 'associating' or working alone, as they wished; above all, it was possible at Wakefield to learn a useful trade. The insistence of these men that everything would be all right if only they could get to Wakefield was pathetic, and I watched it gradually become hopeless. The period served at Wormwood Scrubs by long-sentence men became longer and longer; first it was two years, then two-and-a-half; Wakefield was full up, and the men at the Scrubs would be left to rot.

I do not wish to seem sentimental about the treatment of such prisoners. The great majority of them, although first offenders, had committed some crime which gave Society every excuse for locking them up. We are always being told, however, that the purpose of imprisonment is not so much retribution as reform; not revenge, but cure. Leaving moral considerations aside, this attitude has much to commend it from the practical point of view. Every prisoner eventually gets his release, and it seems only sensible to try and fit him for a better life when he gets out. It is useless to put a man away for a long period, do nothing to change or improve him, and piously hope that by the time he is released he will have magically transformed himself into a good citizen. Men do change in prison, but seldom for the better.

Going to gaol is, in itself, a powerful shock. Suddenly, in the space of a few hours, a man's whole life is changed; he loses friends, possessions and free will and finds himself alone in a hostile place, wearing clothes designed to rob him of his last vestiges of self-respect and eating food which, for the first few days at least, makes him feel ill and depressed. Whatever values he may have had are destroyed; whatever faith he may have had is shaken. If his life is to be rebuilt, the process should begin at that moment.

Since Wormwood Scrubs is sometimes described as a 'hospital' prison, it is perhaps necessary to explain that the hospital block, which contains about 120 beds, is a completely separate entity which serves most of the prisons in England as a treatment centre for minor operations. In contrast to the rest of the prison, which has been condemned as unfit for habitation for many years past, the hospital is new and spotlessly clean. The Principal Medical Officer is an agreeable Irish psychiatrist named Dr Landers, whose office is expensively furnished with deep-pile carpets and contemporary style chairs and desk. Prisoners approach Dr Landers for an interview, having previously removed their shoes, in their stockinged feet across a gleaming expanse of polished tiles. After I had been at Wormwood Scrubs for three or four months, he sent for me. I found him sympathetic and courteous.

We discussed my case, and the possibility of medical or psychiatric treatment, at some length. The Prison Doctor at Winchester, I was not surprised to hear, had expressed the opinion that I was not a suitable subject for treatment. There was a certain irony in this fact, because the psychiatrist who gave evidence at my trial had said that the chance of a successful cure, 'outside', was good. It thus seemed that I had been removed from an environment in which something might have been done for me, and placed in one in which nothing could be done.

Dr Landers, in any case, was not one of those who claimed that there was a psychiatric 'cure' for homosexuality. 'The Freudians,' he explained, 'may think there is, but we're all Jungians here. If a man is so obsessed by his homosexual state that he develops a neurosis about it, we can allay that neurosis and teach him, so to speak, to accept his condition without any severe feeling of guilt; but that's all we can do.'

This sounded like an admirable service for those who were in need of it, but it seemed very strange to me that a man should be sent to prison in order to reconcile himself to the condition which had caused him to be sent there.

'I don't think that's quite what I need,' I said.

'But you have said, if I remember correctly, that you are willing to be cured?'

'Yes, but if there is no cure, surely the question does not arise? Or is there some other method? What about glandular injections, or hormone treatment; is that any good?'

Dr Landers pursed his lips. 'I most certainly wouldn't recommend it,' he said. 'We have tried courses of injections on a couple of sex-cases here, but the results were far from satisfactory. One man came back quite shortly afterwards with a further conviction, and the other has undergone physical

144

changes of a . . . a somewhat alarming nature. I am afraid that research on those lines is not very far advanced yet. It may do some good, but really we don't know enough about it.'

'Well, is there anything else you can suggest?'

'The only thing that might answer, in your case, is a course of analysis and psychotherapy which would, of course, be a very lengthy business lasting perhaps years. Even if we had time, I rather doubt whether it could be carried out satisfactorily in prison. You might, perhaps, consult a psychiatrist about it when you are discharged.'

We were back where we had started. If I had not been sent to prison, I might have been cured.

'There's just one thing,' I said. 'Supposing that I could afford a course of psychotherapy and so on; supposing I found a psychiatrist who was prepared to give it; supposing, even that it worked. What sort of person should I become?'

Dr Landers laughed. 'A very different person, I'm afraid,' he said.

'That's just what I'm afraid of, too.'

'Your whole personality would, of course, be altered.'

'But that,' I suggested, 'might not be a good thing? I'm a writer. For better or for worse, my work depends upon the sort of person that I am.'

'Precisely.'

'You see, I might spend years in having this treatment, and discover in the end that I've become a completely normal, respectable member of Society, but that in the process I've lost all my individuality, and in fact everything that makes it possible for me to earn a living.'

'That, of course, is something which you will have to bear in mind.'

I went away from Dr Landers reflecting that he had, at least, been commendably frank.

*

On fine evenings after tea we used to spend our Association period sitting out in the exercise yard, watching two teams of prisoners playing cricket with an old tennis-ball. We were allowed to take our jackets off, and I found it relaxing and

145

pleasant to sit in the sun with a group of friends, even though the air, as usual at Wormwood Scrubs, was filled with invisible particles of coal-dust which drifted down and covered our faces and hair with a fine greyish film. Sometimes we succeeded in getting one of the newspapers which were issued each day in the proportion of one to every ten men, but usually we just sat and talked.

One evening Dan was telling me about a gang of pick-pockets who used to operate in Petticoat Lane on Sunday mornings. They had an ingenious and successful technique. One of the gang, specially chosen for this accomplishment, would collect a copious mouthful of saliva and squirt it on to the coat-lapel of a passer-by. Another would draw the victim's attention to this and start vigorously mopping at it with his handkerchief, while a third, approaching from behind, would relieve him of his wallet. I accused Dan of making this up.

'No, straight, Pete, they done it for years. Charlie, you remember that lot, don't you?'

'Yes,' said Charlie. 'Known as the Gob Mob, they was.'

'The things one learns in prison!' remarked John. 'Did you know that women shoplifters wear a special kind of knickers called "oyster drawers"? Jimmy told me.'

'Why "oyster"?' I asked.

'I haven't the faintest idea, unless it's because the elastic makes them snap shut after they've popped whatever-it-is into them. Jimmy, why "oyster"?'

'I don't know, we always calls shoplifters "oysters".'

'Not "oysters",' said Dan. 'Hoisters.'

'Oh, how disappointing.'

'It sounds like one of those frightful arguments that go on in the *The Times* correspondence column,' said Basil. 'By the way, has anybody seen *The Times*?'

After some investigation, Vic was discovered sitting on it. Basil spread it out on his knees and became engrossed.

'Have you heard Cokey's latest word?' asked John. Mr Cockayne, in the course of his frequent speeches to the prisoners, was fond of introducing some striking and polysyllabic expression, which never failed to become a catchword. 'He was standing outside his office this morning, trying to attract the attention of the screws on the landing, and of course as usual they all went and hid in the recesses as soon as they heard him bawling. So he went and got the ship's bell that they wake us up with and stood there bashing it backwards and forwards, clang! clang! and no-one took a blind bit of notice, so finally he threw it on the floor and screamed at the top of his voice: WHAT DO YOU THINK I AM, A BLOODY CAMPAN-OLOGIST?'

'I say, Peter, have you seen this?' Basil flung *The Times*, a crushed bundle, into my lap. The names of the members of the Departmental Committee on Homosexuality and Prostitution had been anounced, and *The Times* leader was addressing them in remarkably plain terms:

The official committee to inquire into homosexual offences and prostitution will need unusual courage and unusual common sense. ... The crucial question before the committee is not whether homosexual relations are sinful, but whether the law should punish them as such.

It is agreed that the law must interfere with sexual behaviour in three main instances – where there is assault, where advantage is taken of children or others incapable of giving valid consent, and when there is public indecency. Where relations between persons of the same sex are involved, however, the law goes farther. It punishes severely purely private relations between consenting adult men.

This state of affairs is not merely anomalous. It is widely held to create conditions in which blackmail and provocation can flourish. There is certainly ground for believing (with the recent report of a group of Churchmen) that the state of the law and the publicity attending trials tend to create and maintain 'an aggrieved and self-conscious minority' more convinced than ever of the rightness of their ways.

Forty years ago Havelock Ellis pointed out how strict enforcement of a similar law in Prussia was, by publicity and resentment, greatly enlarging such a minority, whereas in England the problem was dwindling – though it could never wholly disappear – because the law was tacitly falling into desuetude.

Merely to let the law moulder is never a wise course. At the same time, recent attempts to enforce it, where no minors and no public indecency were involved, have compelled the community to examine the question how far it is now justified.

The answer which the committee has to give, at once humane and just, cannot be easy and is bound to be controversial. But it is socially necessary that it should be given.

New subjects for discussion were so rare that all my friends read this article as eagerly as though it personally concerned them. Basil said: 'You know, it really looks as though you've won your battle. With the Church of England, *The Times*, and Sir Robert Boothby on the side of the angels I don't see how the law can help being changed. It'll be a curious feeling, won't it, having been convicted of a crime that no longer exists?'

'Do you think they'll let you out before your time?' asked Dan.

'Not a chance,' I said. 'You have no idea how long it takes for these things to happen.'

A defaulting insurance-broker, who had been eaves-dropping on the conversation, observed in fruity tones: 'The law will never be changed, in my opinion, as long as we have a Queen on the throne.'

We ignored this. 'Can't think why it's a crime anyway,' said Vic. 'I never thought about it much till I came in here, but even I can see the difference between someone like Peter and someone like that horrible Molly.' Molly was a male prostitute who entertained one or two of the 'D' Hall warders in his cell at night. 'Not that Molly does much harm, mind you. The people I hate are the ones that goes after kids.'

'Like me,' said John.

'No, not like you. Yours was sixteen, wasn't he?'

'Yes, but I didn't know, and he looked much older.'

'There you are, you see. You was caught in just the same way as all these blokes who are in for doing a girl under age. Some smashing tart comes wiggling up to them in the boozer, all nylons and high-heeled shoes and paint an inch thick on their mooeys, and says "Hello, handsome; buy me a small port?" Well, nature takes its course, and the next time they sees her she's in the witness-box, wearing a school tunic and all innocent like. Diabolical liberty, I call it.'

'And that, of course,' said Basil, 'is precisely what's going to happen all the time if the law *is* changed. I wonder what the age of consent will be?'

'If you can die for your country at 18 you ought to be old enough to make up your own mind,' said John. I thought it should be 21, because I doubted very much if anyone could be 'corrupted' against their wish or led astray after that age, whereas some men, at 18, were still impressionable adolescents.

'I wasn't,' said Dan.

'No, but then you weren't at a Public School,' Basil pointed out. 'The working classes grow up a great deal quicker than we do, you know. That's why it's such awful nonsense for judges to pretend that the better-class man is the more guilty of the two, in a case like Peter's or John's. I'm quite convinced from what I've seen in here that homosexuality isn't so much a vice of the idle rich as the working man's favourite hobby.'

'Good God!' said the insurance-broker.

'Yes, even with a Queen on the throne,' snapped Basil. 'In any case, there have been plenty of queer Kings of England. What about that William Rufus? And Edward the Second? And did you know that when Elizabeth was succeeded by James the First some naughty Bishop said "The King is dead; long live the Queen"?'

At this moment the cricket-match ended, and a warder shouted to us to return to our cells. We picked up our chairs and walked out of the sunlight, into the stinking gloom of 'D' Hall. Dan and I lingered behind for a moment before going up the iron staircase to our landing.

'I didn't like to say too much out there,' said Dan, 'but I'm so glad about what they put in the paper. You're going to be all right, aren't you? That makes me happy, too.'

'Thanks, Dan.'

He fumbled in his pocket. 'Here, I've got something for you. I pinched it out of the garden while the screws wasn't looking. Make your cell a bit more like home.' He put something into my hand, and we climbed the stairs.

'Good night, Pete. See you in the morning.'

'See you in the morning.'

When I had shut my cell door, I looked at Dan's present. It was a sprig of lavender, and its scent filled the air like a song.

I sat down at the table, holding the lavender in my hand, and thinking how strange it was that these small grey leaves, grimy with the dust of prison, should smell so clean and sweet.

*

Next morning, Dan was waiting for me, as usual, on the exercise yard. He was wearing a clean shirt, a tie which he had made himself, and a pair of trousers with a crease in them, achieved presumably by putting them under his mattress.

'Whatever's happened to you, Dan?' I asked. 'Expecting a visit?'

'No. I been waiting for a visit for the last three weeks, but it don't look like they're bothering to come. I just got sick of being scruffy, that's all.'

'How much longer is it now?'

'Twelve months in December. Pete, I've been thinking.'

'About going out?'

'Yes. I can't stand no more of this. I'm going to find myself a job, and begin all over again.'

'What kind of job?'

'Well, I can drive a lorry. It won't bring in much, I know, but I got to get used to that. I can make do with a few quid a week, if I make up my mind to it; not going after the big money no more. It ain't worth it. I see that now. The penny's dropped. You know what I'm like, Pete; you or anyone else could argue their heart out trying to make me go straight, and it wouldn't do no good, I'm funny that way. It's not that I don't appreciate it, but I just won't be pushed around by no-one, not even you.'

'You make me sound like the Sally Army, Dan. I'm not trying to save your soul, you know; I'm just trying to keep you out of the Moor.'

'Yes, but why should you bother? Nobody's ever bothered with me, and if they have I've usually let them down, that's the honest truth.'

'If I was able to help you in any way, would you let me down too?'

'No,' he said, fiercely. 'I wouldn't. You've been let down quite enough already by people like me. Anyhow, I'm not going to give you a chance, Pete. I've decided to go straight by myself, and I'm going to do it by myself. I don't want to be helped by no-one. I'm going to come along and see you one day and say: "Look, I made it." Then we can be friends, with neither of us feeling that we owes anything to the other. That O.K. by you?'

'Yes,' I said. Dan pulled a piece of bread out of his pocket and threw it to a pigeon, which sidled towards us with its head on one side. 'Scruffy little bastard,' said Dan. 'Looks like it's been crossed with a blackbird. Been too long in the nick.'

*

Bill had decided to re-christen his machine 'Marilyn'. He was scratching the new name carefully on the paintwork with the point of a screwdriver. 'I know it's none of my business,' he remarked, 'but I really must congratulate you on the change you've wrought in that Starling.'

'Do you mean the clean shirt?'

'No, I don't. I mean the whole outlook. It's impressive.'

'I don't think I have much to do with it.'

'Oh, yes. Since you arrived, he's practically unrecognizable. He used to be a horror; never spoke to anyone, except occasionally when he felt like a fight. And so mean!'

'Don't be ridiculous, Bill. He's the most generous person I've ever met. He's always giving me things.'

Bill jabbed me lightly in the ribs with the screwdriver. 'I bet,' he observed, 'you never thought you'd end up being richly kept by a burglar.'

'Are you by any chance going to warn me against him?'

'Certainly not. I think he's a delightful chap, and I see no reason why you shouldn't be very happy together. I don't know what the judge would say; but then I'm not a judge. I'm just a very ordinary man whose views have been changed quite a lot by going to prison. It so happens that I like women – rather too much, as a matter of fact. I wouldn't like it at all if the law applied the same rules to my sex-life as it does to yours. So, as I said before, I congratulate you.'

*

It was not I, however, who made the last and most important change in Dan. It was a little Polish tailor, who had been posted from Winchester. He had brown hair streaked with grey, lustrous brown eyes like those of a mouse, and the most ferocious Cockney accent I have ever heard. 'Moy nyme,' he explained when we first met, 'is Jerzy Poniatowski, but moy mytes calls me Pony.' He had got a short sentence for receiving stolen goods, which he swore he had not known to be 'bent', and when he appeared before the Appeal Court he came within an inch of having his sentence quashed on a technical misdirection. Before getting into trouble he had worked in a London clothing factory and made gentlemen's suits and overcoats at home in the evenings. I introduced him to Dan, who was fascinated by him.

'He's such a funny little tyke, with that "gorblimey" accent and all,' said Dan, 'but he certainly knows his stuff about tailoring. It's interesting, too, when you hear him talk. I never knew there was so much in it.'

Dan had been working in the Tailors' Shop at the Scrubs for nearly two years; but, like all of us, he did his work mechanically and without interest. Fortunately, Jerzy was given the machine next to Dan's. They discussed the finer points of tailoring in whispers all through the working hours, and in the evenings Jerzy would sit drawing endless diagrams on lavatory-paper or in a notebook. Dan's enthusiasm was intense, and I wondered how long it would last.

I asked Jerzy whether he thought Dan would ever make a tailor. 'Blimey, yes,' he said. 'He sews lovely on the machine; all he wants now is some practice in cutting and handsewing. I'll give him a job anytime, anytime at all.'

'I wish you would, Jerzy. You'd be doing more good than you know.'

'Certainly, he's a nice kid and he needs help, doesn't he? I'll teach him all I know, and perhaps he could take a correspondence course as well. Then by the time he gets out he'll be really useful.'

I rather jibbed at suggesting the correspondence course to Dan, but he thought it a splendid idea when it was put to him by Jerzy. He made the necessary application to the Chaplain, and told the Principal Officer in charge of the Tailors' Shop what he had done. The Principal Officer had been in the Prison Service for thirty-odd years; he had played dominoes with murderers in the condemned cell and watched thousands of prisoners come and go (and, quite often, come back again), but Dan's sudden urge to be a tailor must have been unique in his experience. He was flattered when Dan approached him for professional advice, but I think he suspected that there was a catch in it somewhere.

After a few weeks, he was almost proved right. At this time, Dan was making prisoners' jackets, and was earning quite good money on a piece-rate. He discovered, however, that one of the newly arrived prisoners was a Lithuanian tailor who was capable of working at great speed but was only being paid 10d a week, like all men starting a sentence. It seemed to Dan quite wrong that so much work should be done for so little money. An arrangement was made, by which the Lithuanian gave his made-up jackets to Dan in exchange for tobacco, and Dan traded them in to the stores as his own work. Everybody was thus kept happy except the Principal Officer, who found out, as he was bound to do, that Starling was 'fiddling' again.

I went to the Principal Officer and asked him not to punish Dan. I pointed out that his new-found interest in tailoring was the only thing that gave any hope for his future, and that it must at all costs be preserved. A man's life, I said, was more important, even to the Prison Commissioners, than a few pennies. It occurred to me afterwards that I had overplayed this scene rather badly, considering that the Principal Officer knew quite well that Dan was one of his best machinists, and had no intention of losing him. At all events, Dan was let off with a caution.

When I told him what I had done, Dan appeared to be impressed, but rather amused at the idea of my battling with the authorities on his behalf. Like most of the prisoners he was, at heart, afraid of the more senior officials in the prison, whatever he might say about them behind their backs. It had probably never occurred to him that some of them, at least, were reasonable human beings. For the last nineteen years, I suppose, he had been accustomed to equate Authority with petty tyranny, and the habit was by now impossible to break. If I ever suggested to Dan that such-and-such a warder was not a bad sort, he would reply firmly that there was no such thing as a good 'screw', except possibly a dead one. This attitude also extended to the police, the judges, and everyone else in a position of authority: politicians were dishonest charlatans, priests were venial and insincere, doctors didn't know what they were talking about and you couldn't believe a word you read in the papers. He lived in a world of suspicion and fear.

If Dan, and all the men like him, were ever to be useful citizens, somebody should have been trying to break down this attitude and persuading them that authority was not synony-mous with harsh injustice, in the same way that rebellious colonial tribesmen, we are told, must gradually be brought to realize that administrators and police are there for their pro-tection, rather than their subjugation. The only way in which this lesson could be taught in prison was by the example of the men in authority, from the ordinary uniformed 'screw' up to the Principal Governor himself.

The staff of a prison falls into two main and distinct groups. First there are the warders, whose principal responsibility is the keeping of discipline. The pay is reasonably good, but it is not, by its very nature, the kind of occupation likely to attract the best type of man. Promotion is slow, and leads only to the position of Chief Officer, which is subservient to that of Governor. If, as has so often been stated, the twin objects of imprisonment are deterrence and reform, the role of the warder is uniquely concerned with deterrence. The propa-ganda which is used to attract recruits to the Prison Service apparently gives a rather different impression. I have spoken to several young trainee-warders who had entered the Service hoping that it would give them scope for some form of welfare work or social first-aid, but when they discovered that their duties consisted mainly of marching the prisoners around and shouting at them, they resigned in disappointment. Far from being expected to take an intelligent interest in the problems of an individual prisoner, the warders are not supposed to know what any man is 'in' for and are not allowed to talk to him except in the strict line of duty.

Given these facts, it is astonishing that the Prison Service should contain so many decent, good-hearted men. In every prison there are, of course, a few cranks and bullies, who are quite obvious to everyone and should have been weeded out long ago. There are also a great many who merely do what they are paid to do, in a kind of bovine trance-state which is strikingly like that of some of the long-term prisoners. They become glassy-eyed automata, thinking only of overtime and the retirement pension. They are probably no better and no worse, as guards, than the electronic eyes and mechanical computers which could so easily replace them. Fortunately, in addition to the bullies and the robots, there exists a small body of warders – almost, one might say, an underground movement – which contrives to take a real interest in the prisoners, and which is perhaps the most potent force for the reform of criminals which exists to-day.

I wish I could say the same of the Principal Governors, Deputy and Assistant Governors, for it is in their hands that the real power lies. I have experience at first hand of only two prisons, and it is conceivable that they may not be typical in this respect; but I can only write of the Governors whom I know.

None of them, I think, had been 'through the ranks' of the Prison Service. They had entered it, in middle age, after a career in the Army or in the Colonial Service, and their whole attitude to the prisoners reflected these twin backgrounds. Wormwood Scrubs, for example, under the leadership of Major Ben Grew, was run as a kind of caricature of the military life. Three of his subordinates, to my knowledge, had brought with them to the Scrubs a typical 'sahib' attitude towards men of colour; and the colour discrimination in the prison was one of its most nauseating features. There did not seem to me to be the slightest attempt by the authorities to discover, understand or grapple with the problems presented by the 1,000 individuals in their charge; the men were simply herded together like sheep for whatever period the judges had been pleased to allot to them.

Officially, any prisoner had the right to see the Governor whenever he had a complaint or a request to make. In practice, this was made as difficult as possible. When a prisoner did succeed in obtaining an interview with the Governor, he found him hedged about with assistants and officers, so that it was impossible to speak freely. The interview was conducted in a court-martial atmosphere, in which it was made quite plain to the prisoner that his word would not be taken against that of an officer, and that any complaint considered frivolous would land him in serious trouble. Complaints about the food, for example, were therefore rather less frequent than one would have expected. We all knew that, if we complained, not only would nothing be done, but we should make ourselves unpopular with the authorities, who had a hundred petty ways of getting even with us. If this idea appears exaggerated, I can only say that on two occasions while I was at Wormwood Scrubs a prisoner who had made a complaint against an officer was later 'discovered' to be harbouring a hacksaw-blade in his cell. It was always the same hacksaw-blade, and I have been told that it turns up remorselessly in the cell of any man who makes himself sufficiently unpopular. In each case the 'discovery' is followed by a sentence of bread-and-water and the loss of a few weeks' remission.

I only had one serious encounter with Major Grew, which concerned the allowance of letters. In contrast with the regime of Major Paton-Walsh at Winchester, who prevented me from receiving my letters and hinted strongly that they were from men masquerading as women, the situation at Wormwood Scrubs was, to begin with, more easy. During the first few months of my sentence I received a large number of 'unofficial' letters – a relaxation of the rules which enabled me, to some extent at least, to judge how I stood with the friends whom I had left behind. This, however, was before the arrival of a new Assistant Governor, who seemed to me to be unduly keen to prevent prisoners from receiving letters in excess of their meagre ration of one every two weeks.

He was a huge, unhappy-looking man, dressed, like all Prison Governors, in a dirty mackintosh and a hat with a brim turned up in front. He was always padding up and down the staircases and along the landings, so that the burglars, whenever they saw him, were apt to remark that the doss-house must have burned down. At night he used to visit various men in their cells and talk to them. I believe he meant this kindly, and he was at least the only official who attempted to make contact with the men in his charge. His manner, however, seems to have been so clumsy and tactless that he only succeeded in arousing the resentment of the prisoners.

On several occasions I was 'called-up' by this gentleman in order to be told that a letter had come for me from Miss So-and-so, 'whoever she may be', and that it would be sent back to her unread because it was surplus to my entitlement. Once or twice I managed to get the letter by pointing out, quite truthfully, that it was a reply to one which I had written.

All the letters written and received by us were, of course, read by one of the warders. Although this was nearly always done in a humane and liberal manner, the knowledge that someone else was reading our letters inevitably had a deadening effect on our correspondence. I was fortunate in having several friends who were capable of writing entertaining letters even when they were being most carefully impersonal, but the majority of prisoners received only brief reports on the health of their relations, written in stilted, formal terms as though the writers were uneasily aware that someone was looking over their shoulders. The result was that letters, so eagerly awaited, were nearly always a disappointment when they arrived, and what was not said in them became even more important than the sparse news which they contained.

It would be hard to exaggerate the importance of the part which letters played in our lives. They were our only link with the future, and in most cases the link was sadly slender. One inarticulate letter every two weeks is not much of a help, for example, in keeping alive a marriage which is threatened by a separation lasting several years, and it was pitiful to watch the misunderstandings and suspicions growing up in the minds of men whose wives were either too busy or too ill-educated to write them the kind of letters which they needed to get. A delay of a few days in answering a letter was enough, in our surroundings, to start an avalanche of jealousy and mistrust.

The visits which we were allowed to receive once a month were necessarily brief, and hampered by the presence of a warder. In addition to these, a few prisoners were seen occasionally in their cells by voluntary Prison Visitors – an admirable form of service which could do much good if it were organized on better lines. Unfortunately a prisoner who applied for these visits was obliged to take pot-luck and was by no means sure of getting a congenial visitor. Most of the men hesitated to expose themselves to visits from a stranger who was more likely than not to be an elderly person bent on delivering moral lectures to what American advertisers call a 'captive audience'. The visitors themselves were handicapped by the prison rules, which forbade them to discuss a man's crime with him – a subject which would have to be tackled sooner or later if anything constructive was to come out of their meetings.

A constructive approach to the problems of crime was, however, the last thing that one expected to find at Wormwood Scrubs. For this, I do not think it unfair to give some of the blame to the Governor, Major Grew, who for some reason has always managed to escape criticism, although it is generally accepted that the Scrubs, of which he had been in charge for many years, is the worst prison to which first offenders can be sent.

Since my release, I have heard many glowing reports of Major Grew from penal-reformers and others who interest themselves in Her Majesty's Prisons. It is generally accepted that Wormwood Scrubs is the worst place to which a first offender can be sent, and that its sanitary conditions would, to quote the Earl of Huntingdon, disgrace a Hottentot village. But this, apparently, is not to be laid at the door of Major Grew, who has been in charge of the place for many years. When the praises of Maidstone Prison are sung, as they are so often and so loudly, the credit for its splendour is heaped upon Mr Vidler, the Governor; but when the stink of Wormwood Scrubs reaches the nostrils of the House of Lords, it seems to be generally assumed that no blame can be attached to Major Grew.

Visitors to the Scrubs were, of course, never allowed to

wander into the more unsavoury parts, in which we spent most of our time. If anybody was coming to see the workshops, half a dozen men would be detailed to scrub out the lavatories (thus causing even further frustration to those who wished to use them) and, in the case of really 'nosey' visitors like the Howard League for Penal Reform, to paint the doors and polish the brasswork. There was one hilarious occasion when the Mayor and Mayoress of West Acton, with a posse of local notabilities, visited the prison. In case of unfortunate encounters, all the prisoners were locked in their cells with the exception of a score or two of 'Leaders', who were mostly policemen fallen from grace or similar types who had ingratiated themselves with the authorities. These men were all fitted out with specially-made new uniforms, clean shirts and fresh armbands emblazoned with the name of their particular responsibility, such as 'LIBRARY', 'CHURCH OF ENGLAND' or 'DRAINS'. I do not know whether they were allowed to talk to the visitors, but they must have looked extremely decorative. The guests, apparently, had expressed a wish to see the various articles and works of art made by the happy and industrious prisoners in their spare time, and we all wondered where these were to come from. The instructors in the Tailors' Shop, however, stepped into the breach by producing one or two highly professional examples of garment manufacture; the art-class did its garish best, and although we were never allowed to see the resultant exhibition we strongly suspected that most of the items arrived in a van labelled 'LCC' which we saw parked in the yard.

*

June ... July ... August ... September. I was half-way through my sentence. 'It'll go quicker now,' said Dan. 'You're going down-hill.' But the days seemed just as long. I could not read in the evenings any more, because in addition to our daily work we were now compelled to sew mailbags in our cells. It was a maddening, useless task, sitting there in the dull glow of a 40-watt bulb screwed up high in the ceiling, eternally stitching away at the tough canvas, eight stitches to the inch. The Chaplain said that the system had been introduced because some of the prisoners had complained that they had not enough to do in the evenings; it was purely voluntary, and no-one who had anything better to do would be punished if he failed to carry out the weekly task. Several prisoners took his advice and stopped sewing their bags. After they had been stripped and examined by the Medical Officer to see whether they were fit enough for bread-and-water, they were brought before the Governor. He let most of them off with a warning that they must stitch their quota of mailbags in future. We did not believe anything the Chaplain told us after that.

When I had been an undergraduate at Oxford I had spent much of my time in interminable conversations, discussing every conceivable problem of the world in a room thick with smoke and littered with empty glasses and unwashed cups, until the dawn came creeping over Magdalen Bridge. But I do not remember any conversations more intense and absorbing than those I had in prison, with Bob the scientist, John the businessman, Vic the river-pilot and Charlie, Dan and Jimmy, the burglars. We talked about politics and sex and religion and art and war and the best way to blow the back off a Chubb safe, but in the end we always returned to the subjects of punishment and reform. This hardly sounds credible, but it is true; I heard more sensible suggestions from those criminals than I have heard from any penologist or politician since my release.

Whether they intended to 'go straight' or not, none of them believed that they would be better men for their stay in prison. It had made them feel that they were outlaws, and would remain so. Those who had decided to abandon crime had not done so because of any moral awakening, but simply because they could not stand the thought of coming back to prison again. On the face of it, this sounds like powerful proof of the deterrent effect of imprisonment, but I am not so sure. It is one thing to make good resolutions when you are sitting in Wormwood Scrubs; it is quite another to come out into an unfriendly world with no job, no home, nothing in your pocket but fifteen shillings from the Discharged Prisoners' Aid Society, and no friends except other criminals.

The main complaint which these men had against the prison

was not the discipline or the filthy sanitary conditions, but the fact that no attempt was being made to fit them for life 'outside'. The work which they did in the shops was monotonous and almost useless from the point of view of a future career; they were taught to do one thing and did it all the time, year in and year out. The Principal Officer in the Tailors' Shop, Mr Heath, and his two instructors did what they could to help Dan and others, who were genuinely interested, to gain a wider knowledge of the trade, but their efforts were unofficial and exceptional. I believe that they would have been only too pleased to organize evening classes for men who wished to take up tailoring on their release, but the higher authorities did not seem to be interested in the idea.

There were evening classes, of course, but they were perfunctory and uninspired. The instructors frequently failed to turn up, and from the fragments of lectures on 'Civics', 'Science' and 'Current Affairs' which I heard the standard was deplorably low. The handicraft classes were run according to the most extraordinary rule. If a man made, say, a leather handbag, and wished to send it home, he had to buy it from the prison authorities at a price assessed by them – not the cost of the materials, be it noted, but an artificial price determined by a committee of the Chaplain and various Governors. If he was willing to pay this price, the money had to be sent in by a friend or relative. The prisoner, of course, never saw this money, which was placed in his 'property', but there were endless difficulties. Vic, for example, made a handbag which was given a value of 35/- (the materials having cost approximately 4/6). 'My Shirley Rose' sent him the money, but it was sent back by one of the subsidiary Governors, who accused Vic of having acquired it by trafficking in tobacco with other prisoners. That was the end of evening classes, as far as Vic was concerned.

But the thing that really crippled the evening classes, together with reading, writing, painting or any other attempt by the prisoners to improve their education, was the weekly quota of mailbags. This unpaid labour occupied about an hour of our leisure time every night. It severely curtailed my own reading and writing, and Dan, Charlie, and Jimmy, who were slow readers, stopped patronizing the library altogether.

We often discussed what an ideal prison would be like, supposing that such a place could exist. The Chaplain to the Commissioners, an eloquent Welshman, was fond of pointing out in his sermons the horrors of prison life in other countries; but we knew better, because there were a good many prisoners who had 'done time' in various foreign gaols. My Canadian friend at Winchester had already told me that at Sing-Sing he had been allowed to have his own typewriter, on which he wrote short stories which he was permitted to sell to magazines; at Wormwood Scrubs one was not even allowed to have a fountain-pen sent in, and the rules about taking out written work on discharge were ludicrously obscure. Bill, my companion on the button-hole machine, had spent a few weeks in the prison of La Santé in Paris, where, he told me, work was commissioned by outside firms who paid good wages, out of which the prisoners were able to buy a wide choice of food and drink. The Lithuanian tailor told us that in Communist gaols the prisoners were permitted a monthly parcel, containing food and cigarettes, and that it was possible to earn remission by extra work.

This was a system which had already been suggested, rather surprisingly, by Dan. His idea was that in certain cases a convicted man should be sentenced, not to so many years' imprisonment, but to a stated amount of work: a thousand mailbags, or ten thousand pairs of socks, or preferably something which could be sold outside the prison. In this way, the men would be given a real incentive to hard work; the prisons would eventually become less crowded; and the money earned by the prisoners could be used for their rehabilitation, both directly and indirectly. Each man would have a small nest-egg to take out with him, and deductions could be made each week to help with the salaries of instructors and the provision of lecture-rooms and workshops. Furthermore, a man who had caused a financial loss to someone by his crime would have an opportunity of paying it off, at least in part, by his own efforts.

The wastage of earning-power in Wormwood Scrubs seemed to be almost deliberate. Men who already possessed some useful training were very seldom given a job in which they could practise it. There was no shortage of plumbers, builders, and cooks, but they were not to be found in the Works party or in the cookhouse. Some of the allocations were so eccentric that they could only be ascribed to a macabre sense of humour on the part of someone in authority. A horrible creature who had pleaded insanity when charged with raping his own children was given the job of looking after prisoners who went to see the psychiatrist. A soldier, found guilty of mutilating an African suspect in Kenya, was put to work in the operating theatre. An ex-Guards officer, much publicized during his trial as a friend of the Royal Family, was put in charge of the sink where the sample bottles of urine were washed. A man who had killed two girls by administering an aphrodisiac to them was immediately given a 'Red Band' and seconded to the hospital.

An establishment run on such lines was obviously not going to fit anybody for a better life. We did what we could to help each other, but it was not much. Jerzy, the little Pole, used to give Dan tailoring lessons every evening, but after a few months he was sent away to another prison. Dan then applied for permission to take a correspondence course. Every conceivable obstacle was put in his way. One of the warders, nominally in charge of education, told him: 'This is a very expensive course, too expensive to waste on anybody like you.' Dan pointed out that if he was forced to go back to housebreaking and received a further sentence, he would cost the country a great deal more than the fees for the course. He took his request to a higher level, and after a long delay was told that the time he still had to do was too short to allow him to complete the course. He then began all over again, with a request for a shorter course. I never heard the end of the story, because I was released before he had had any reply.

*

Two things kept me going. One was the visit, every three weeks, of Lord Pakenham, who was preparing a report for the Nuffield Foundation on the Causes of Crime. He must have exhausted my views on this subject during the first few visits, but he kept on coming for as long as he was able. Sitting with him there in a room without a warder, in the dingy grey suit which I had worn for six months, with my hands scarred by the mailbag needle and my fingernails black with ingrained dirt, I could feel that I was still a person. I can never repay him for what he did for me during those months.

The other thing that armed me against the world of prison was the feeling which the warder at Winchester had expressed so long ago: 'There's always someone worse off than you.' I found it impossible to pity myself when I was surrounded by so much tragedy and degradation. I looked at the old man who sat opposite me at meals; he was 72, and had been sentenced to seven years' imprisonment for his first offence. While he was on bail, he had had an accident and had been blinded in one eye. He was unable to read, so he just sat staring at the wall. He had a calm and beautiful face, deeply lined with age. He said to me: 'I am quite content. When you are as old as I am, you might as well be here as anywhere else.'

He was not the oldest. There was a man of 82, who was so crippled with rheumatism that when he arrived the other prisoners had to undress him and put his uniform on him. I do not know what his crime had been, but he was, in effect, sentenced to death. He died after a few weeks, in the prison hospital. The man who had poisoned two girls helped to lay him out.

I talked to a boy of 22 who had been sentenced to death for murder, and had spent three months in the condemned cell while his case was considered by the Lords. He told me how they had taken away his shoelaces and the buttons off his coat, and watched him day and night in case he killed himself. There were three things he remembered about the cell: the crucifix over the bed, the door that led to the execution room, and the grating through which he was allowed to speak to his mother.

I met a man who had been flogged at Dartmoor: the worst thing, he said, was the way the 'cat' curled round you and bit into the right side of your chest. I met wicked men and foolish men, and cowards and men whose courage made me feel ashamed, and from each of them I gained a particle of strength, or tolerance, or compassion. I saw much to make me angry, but much, too, that made me glad to be a member of the human race. I felt, almost for the first time, that I was a part of these people, that we were all involved in each other's happiness, and sorrows, and meannesses and sudden, unaccountable bursts of joy. When someone was released we all shared a little of his freedom; when somebody killed himself, we all shared a portion of his death. I learned for the first time the meaning of those great, ringing words which I had known since childhood: 'No man is an island, entire of himself . . . therefore send not to know for whom the bell tolls; it tolls for thee.' I saw that my whole life had been a longing to be part of the world, with all its squalor and its laughter and its tears.

*

It was impossible for me to know what my future would be. The *Daily Mail* had dismissed me when I was convicted, and I did not know whether I would be able to get another job in Fleet Street. From the sparse quota of letters and visits which I was allowed to receive, I gathered that I still had many friends, and that many people whom I had not known before had expressed their willingness to help me. In November, when Edward Montagu was released from Wakefield, I heard that he had been welcomed back by almost everybody, but I could hardly believe that this would happen in my own case. I remembered that I had admitted, in the witness-box, that I was a homosexual. It had seemed to be the right thing to do at the time, but I began to wonder now what effect it would have upon my future. Although I had reacted strongly against it at the time, I was haunted by the suggestion of the Governor at Winchester that I would have to go abroad, change my name, and behave like a furtive outcast for the rest of my life.

Winter came, bringing with it leaking roofs and a flurry of snow on the exercise yard. We began to look forward to Christmas. There was a man in 'D' Hall who made paper flowers; he sat on the floor of his cell night after night, crimping and twisting crêpe-paper carnations and roses and chrysanthemums. Others made garlands and chains from tissue paper and glue, and painted signs in fancy lettering wishing us a Merry Christmas. The food-ration became noticeably more meagre, and the men who had been in prison for more than a year explained that the cooks were beginning to save up for an outsize Christmas dinner.

On the pay-day before Christmas we were given a bonus, according to the length of time which we had done. I received an extra 1s. 6d. with which I bought a packet of Woodbines. We were all rich and reckless, and gave each other presents. The old man Ted, who had stolen the perambulator, redoubled his efforts at scrounging in the Tailors' Shop. On Christmas Eve we concocted an enormous gift stocking inscribed with his name, containing a weird assortment of 'roll-ups', sweets, matches, a clean shirt, and a pair of socks. There were 'joke' presents in it, too; some of the cigarettes contained horsehair or feathers, trouser-buttons were substituted for wine-gums, and a bottle labelled Vaseline Hair Tonic was filled with water. We prevailed upon the Principal Officer to present the stocking to Ted, who fell on it savagely, his eyes watering with anticipation. He smoked the horsehair cigarettes without any apparent discomfort, and sold the 'hair tonic' for a quarter of an ounce of tobacco to a friend, who, as he said later, 'bloody near killed him' when he discovered the deception. Ted, however, had the last laugh, because he had already smoked the tobacco by this time.

Bill and I festooned our button-hole machines with a strip of rag on which we had chalked: 'A Merry Yuletide to all our Customers.' We also put out a Christmas Box, hoping that someone would be hysterical enough to put something in it, but all we collected was a packet of cigarette-papers which turned out to have been cut out of a toilet-roll, and five Woodbines. These were given to us by a young soldier who had gone berserk in the Canal Zone and received seven years for shooting his sergeant; we knew he could not really afford this rich gift, so we bought an equivalent quantity of Nut Milk chocolate and gave it to him.

I received twenty-five Christmas cards from a diverse assortment of friends, including a former charlady, two Peers, a correspondent on *The Times*, a farmer, a Harley Street surgeon, and a barmaid. With these, I decorated my cell.

The ground floor of the Hall, where we ate our meals, was a fantastic sight. There were artificial flowers everywhere, and on Christmas Day the tables were covered with old sheets, which gave them a most luxurious air. Paper-chains were festooned from wall to wall, and those over our table had been augmented by Dan, who had contrived some striking garlands by an ingenious manipulation of torn-up toilet-rolls, glue and red ink. He had been very shocked on the previous Christmas, apparently, to discover that the decorations in 'D' Hall consisted mainly of pieces of the *News of the World*, stained green.

Christmas dinner was quite unlike any other meal of the year. The helpings were enormous, the food queasily rich in comparison with the normal diet, and, as a final gastronomic touch, we were each given a mug of sugared tea. Major Grew stood around beaming, and I felt that we were supposed to burst into 'For He's a Jolly Good Fellow'. Resisting this temptation, we ate as much as we could and rolled the rest up in our handkerchiefs, so that we could eat it in peace in our cells during the next few days. We all felt rather ill next morning, and were not really surprised to hear that one prisoner, no doubt overcome by the gruesome bonhomie of it all, had hanged himself during the night.

I had always told myself that Christmas was the last milestone on the road, and that once it was over I would begin, as the prisoners used to say, to pack. Actually, the last ten weeks of my sentence were by far the worst. The reason for this was purely physical. Although the workshop was steam-heated almost to the point of suffocation, the cells were devoid of any heating at all. There was a small grating in each cell which was supposed to be connected to a circulating system of warm air, but nothing whatever came out of it. It was freely admitted by all the prison officials that the heating arrangements had been out of action for years, but nobody did anything to put them right. The Prison Commissioners, apparently, had adopted their usual attitude of pious hand-wringing and pleaded poverty. Neither Major Grew nor Dr Landers ever visited the cells, and the warders were muffled up in military greatcoats and gloves. The prisoners, still wearing the clothes in which they had sweltered during the summer, had to keep warm as best they could.

I used to sleep in my underwear, shirt and trousers, with

the rest of my clothes piled on my bed in a heap which was loosely held together by tucked-in mailbags. In spite of this, I developed chilblains which made my fingers swell up and crack like beef sausages too rapidly fried. Several prisoners told me that they had been to see the Prison Doctor with this complaint, but had received no treatment. The best cure, I was told by one of the burglars, was to soak a piece of rag in urine and wrap it round the affected part. He added that I might not fancy the idea, but it worked. I tried it, and it did.

In January I was transferred, for meals and Association, to a building known to the authorities as the Old Recreation Hut, and to us as the Old Rec. The wind whistled round and through this ancient hovel with a shrill persistence, reducing us all to a shivering huddle of creatures who would not have been out of place at Belsen. We hunched over the lukewarm waterpipes, blowing on our hands and trying to cover our knees with the thin grey capes provided for outdoor wear. There were no lavatories in the Old Rec, and anyone who wanted to relieve himself had to ask the warder on duty to let him out. When perhaps a dozen had applied, the warder would unlock the door and the men, watched by a 'Leader', would scuttle out into the exercise yard to squat on latrines whose plumbing-system had long since frozen up, and whose seats were often an inch deep in snow.

The Old Rec will always be, for me, a vision of Hell. The wireless loudspeakers, roaring out distorted dance music, made conversation impossible. The lights were dim and un-shaded. The smell of sour food and sweaty feet hung over every-thing like a fog, and everywhere one looked one saw men sitting there, hunched in their capes, their eyes blank, waiting, waiting.

In January, too, the New System began. As we understood it, the theory was that Wormwood Scrubs was gradually to be transformed into something on the lines of Wakefield: a place where men like Dan, who by this time had been in prison for 30 months, would at last have the opportunity of acquiring that 'training for freedom' so glibly advertised by the Prison Commissioners. Mr Cockayne, asking us for our co-operation, told us that the scheme would prove entirely to our advantage in the end. We were all moved to different cells several times, so that 'D' Hall presented the appearance of a demented game of General Post. In the re-shuffle, I contrived to spend four nights in a cell in which the heating actually worked. It was rather like a Turkish bath, but dirtier, because all the hot air which should have been distributed between the 88 cells on the landing was diverted into this one, bringing with it large amounts of brick-dust and soot.

When I left Wormwood Scrubs in March the other prisoners were still waiting to discover the advantages of the new system. The only results, up to then, were that we worked for an extra two hours a day at the same rate of pay, and that our exercise time was cut down from the statutory hour to a bare twenty minutes. There was no sign of any of the privileges to which the long-sentence men would have become entitled if there had been room for them at Wakefield: no vocational training, no freedom of Association, no home leave during the last months of their time.

There were only 28 days in February, but they seemed like 28 years. Someone had sent me a calendar for Christmas, and every night I pencilled out the date.

The Discharged Prisoners' Aid Society asked me whether I needed any assistance on my release.

The Chaplain looked at my notebooks to see whether I had written in them anything obscene or prejudicial to prison discipline.

Jimmy said: 'Try to do something for us when you get out, Pete; we can't do nothing for ourselves.'

It was my last day.

The exercise yard looked just the same. The two crooked businessmen were still walking around with rapid strides, booming at each other. 'You see the one on the left?' asked Basil. 'Well, he's selling a Rolls-Bentley he hasn't got to the one on the right for £2,000 that *he* hasn't got either.'

'How many more hours?' the burglars inquired.

A warder to whom I had never spoken before shook my hand and said: 'I hope very sincerely that all goes well with you from now on.'

I said good-bye to Dan Starling.

*

That night I lay on my hard mattress for the last time and tried to gather together all the jig-saw pieces of experience and understanding which I had collected, so that I could take them out with me in the morning. I marshalled, re-arranged and sorted them in turn, trying to fit them together in a way that had value and meaning for me, if for no-one else.

In prison I had known hatred, laughter, pity, and love. I had learned to know more about my fellow-men than I had ever done before, and I believed that this knowledge would help me to know myself.

I considered the man whose name was written on the card outside the door: 2737, Wildeblood, due for release to-morrow morning, and wondered what kind of person he was. In my imagination, the cell became filled with shadowy figures in wigs and robes. I could hear a rich, sneering voice:

'Ladies and Gentlemen of the Jury, it is the submission of the prosecution – and a submission which, however regrettable, you may feel obliged to accept – that the accused Peter Wildeblood is a man who, during the last twelve calendar months, has consistently shown by his actions and his demeanour that he is in no way capable of profiting by the lesson which Society, in its wisdom, has seen fit to visit upon him.

'I will not take up your time, members of the Jury, by dwelling upon the sordid and deplorable catalogue of his activities. I will merely remind you that he has failed, totally failed, to take advantage of the unique opportunities for the reconstruction of his life and his outlook which exist, as we all know, in Her Majesty's Prisons.

'This man has shown no jot or tittle of remorse, members of the Jury. He has maintained an attitude throughout which you may think is less appropriate to a convicted criminal than to a prisoner of war. An even more revolting feature of his behaviour, in the submission of the Crown, is – and you must forgive me for speaking frankly, Ladies and Gentlemen of the Jury, but we must not flinch from our duty in these matters – an even more revolting feature is the fact that, during his time in prison, he has persistently associated with persons who are infinitely his social inferiors. In the circumstances there is only one verdict which you can give, and I hope you will give it after long scrutiny and careful consideration. That verdict is: Guilty.'

There was a rustle of silk. The jury, who were sitting uncomfortably crammed together on my wash-stand, rose to their feet like puppets on a string. 'Don't the jury wish to retire?' asked the judge.

'Good gracious, no!'

'It's disgusting!'

'There's no smoke without fire!'

'I read it in the paper!' A big blob of spit ran down the windscreen.

'Order, order!' screamed the judge, putting his ear trumpet to his lips and blowing a shrill blast. 'Are you agreed upon your verdict?'

'Of course we are. Guilty. With a strong recommendation to no mercy.'

'Good. I mean yes. Prisoner at the bar, did you hear what they said? Have you anything to say before the sentence of the court is passed upon you?'

But I was not listening. They were only voices, and they could never hurt me any more. I was as detached as a passenger in an aeroplane.

'Wakey-wakey!' shouted a warder through the spyhole. 'It's come at last!'

It was Tuesday, March the eighth. In an hour I should be free. I washed, shaved, collected my belongings, and tore up my calendar. The other prisoners' cells had not yet been unlocked. I walked past the closed doors, thinking of the men who lay behind them. I handed in my blankets, my sheets, my pillow-slip, my brushes, my plate, and my drinking-mug, and my book of rules for the guidance of Convicted Prisoners, Male. I took off the prison clothes and put on my own. I made up a bundle of letters and books to take with me. Two other men were being released that morning; a wizened, red-haired taxi-driver, and a young man in a handpainted tie and gumboots. We sat in the Reception block drinking tea and eating porridge. It was part of the prison lore that a man who left his plate of porridge would return some day to finish it.

At ten minutes to eight the gate was opened. The early shift of warders were coming on duty. Many of them had been my friends, and I shook hands with half a dozen of them. Then I walked out through the gate.

I had never really believed that this would be the end, or even the beginning of a new chapter. It was merely a part of the story which had been implicit in me from the day when I was born; as much a part as the knock on the door when I was arrested, or the moment when, as a child, I realized that I was different from the rest. I could not stop the pages from turning, or close the book. I had chosen to be myself, and I must go on to the end; there must be no abdication, no regret. The world knew what I was, and would make its judgements accordingly, but I could make no concessions to its opinion. 'Simply the thing I am,' I told myself, 'shall make me live.' In a world of hypocrites, I would at least be honest.

For the first few days, I thought that people were looking at me; then I realized that I was flattering myself. I had forgotten that free men and women looked at each other in this way, just as I had forgotten that trees had a clean, green smell and that Virginia cigarettes tasted of damp hay. I wondered what it would be like to come out of prison after a five-year sentence. Even to me, the world was strange and a little frightening; the traffic roared and pounced, the colours of women's dresses, flowers and neon signs jabbed the nerves of my eyes, and music had a new, rich texture as tangible as fur or silk. I woke at dawn, and began to long for bed at dinner-time. When I saw my first egg, I was stricken with awe at the impregnable perfection of its shape, so that I hardly dared to crack it with my spoon. When I saw my first daffodil, I felt like weeping.

My friends said: 'In a few weeks you will have forgotten it all. It will fade from your mind like a bad dream. It's over and done with now, and nobody wants to remember it.' They meant to be kind, but I knew that they were wrong. I could never forget. I would always carry with me, like a hidden scar, the memory of what I had seen. From now on, perhaps, I could never be wholly happy; but at the same time I could never be wholly selfish or consumed with pity for myself, because wherever I went I should be haunted by the faces, savage or resigned or drained of hope, of those hundreds of men so much less fortunate than myself. Society might have succeeded in forgetting them, but I never could. I knew what it was like to be a criminal, to know that everything you did would be misunderstood or used as evidence against you, so that you just drifted, hopelessly, from one prison sentence to the next. I knew something of the bitter rage which wells up in a man's mind during the long cold nights, when he thinks of the punishment which Society, with icy impartiality, is exacting from his wife and children. I knew the dreadful isolation of the prisoner, meticulously deprived of every contact with the world into which, one day, he will be released. I knew how it felt to be a member of a minority, under-privileged even in gaol because of the shape of one's nose or the colour of one's skin.

But, for the time being, my main concern was with the problem of my own future. The classic pattern, which I was determined not to follow, was that of Oscar Wilde: the flight abroad, the assumption of a new name, the eventual death in sterile obscurity. Such a course may have been inevitable for Wilde, but it seemed to me a betrayal of everything in which I believed; it would, moreover, award the final victory to those who had tried so hard to destroy me.

While I was in prison I had written to the Home Secretary, asking for permission to give evidence to the Committee on Homosexual Offences. This permission was granted, but the Committee decided to wait until my release before calling me as a witness, so that I might give my views more freely. I had volunteered to do this because I thought there were probably very few other men who were able or willing to put forward the viewpoint of an admitted homosexual. Most of the evidence, I imagined, would be of a theoretical nature, given by psychiatrists, clergymen and lawyers whose only experience of the problem was of the 'exposed ninth' – the untypical percentage of cases in which mental illness or legal proceedings were involved.

I discovered, however, that I was by no means alone. A number of men holding positions of trust and responsibility, against whose names there had never been a breath of scandal, had offered to give evidence – if necessary, in public. This seemed to me an act of high courage. It was easy for me to speak for the homosexuals, because my admission that I was one of them had received the most widespread publicity; I had nothing further to lose. These others were risking everything to do what they believed to be right. They knew that, once they had appeared before the Committee, their names would be known to the police; and, if no change was made in the law, that their lives would be made intolerable. They had no illusions on this point. They realized that a decision by the Committee to leave the law as it was would be followed, immediately, by a savage and merciless 'purge' of all known homosexuals, in which they would be the first to suffer.

I am not suggesting that the police would be so childish as to indulge in an orgy of revenge. The explanation is much more straightforward than that. In Wormwood Scrubs I had had the opportunity of talking to a number of policemen who had been convicted of various offences, and they all told me the same story. Promotion in the Police Force, they said, depended very largely on the number of convictions secured. In each police station there is, apparently, a kind of score-board on which the convictions obtained by each officer are recorded. It is the number which counts, not the gravity of the offences concerned; and, as one of the ex-detectives at Wormwood Scrubs remarked to me, it is very much easier to arrest a homosexual than a burglar. A policeman whose score is lagging behind that of his colleagues can always catch up by going to the nearest public lavatory, or merely by smiling at someone in the street. By various promises, the arrested man can usually be persuaded to plead guilty; if he does not, his word is unlikely to be taken against that of a police officer. Mr E. R. Guest, the magistrate at West London, was reported recently as saying that his court alone dealt with 600 such cases every year. This grotesque mis-statement was much quoted as a sign of the decadence of the age and the prevalence of homosexuality; Mr Guest's subsequent explanation that he had in fact said sixty cases a year went almost unnoticed. There is little doubt, however, that prosecutions for homosexual acts are on the increase, and for a very good reason. As one man said to me in prison: 'Why should they climb a tree to catch a burglar, when they can pick up people of our sort like apples off the ground?'

Whatever the decisions of the Committee may be, they will still have to be accepted or rejected, in the end, by the opinion of ordinary men and women. It is not a question which is usually discussed, and it may therefore be rather difficult to obtain a fair sample of public opinion. The question, in its simplest form, is: Should the law be amended so that the acts of consenting adults, in private, are no longer regarded as a crime?

I believe that it should, but my opinion is naturally coloured by the fact that I am one of those whose lives would be made easier by such a change. This, however, is not the only consideration on which I base my view. I am thinking of the thousands of others who, even if they never come into direct conflict with the law, are condemned to a life of concealment and fear. Fear is a terrible emotion; it is like a black frost which blights and stunts all the other qualities of a man. If half a million men, who are good citizens in every other respect, are to remain under this perpetual shadow, I believe that Society itself will be the ultimate loser.

The right which I claim for myself, and for all those like me, is the right to choose the person whom I love. I have my own standards of morality about this; and they are not so very different from those of normal men and women. I do not wish to hurt another person; and for that reason I would not willingly persuade anyone to join me in a way of life which, whatever happens to the law, will always present grave and painful difficulties. I have no wish to corrupt the young, nor to convert to homosexuality – even if this were possible, which I doubt – any man who was lucky enough to possess normal instincts. I seek only to apply to my own life the rules which govern the lives of all good men: freedom to choose a partner and, when that partner is found, to live with him discreetly and faithfully.

Discretion and fidelity are, however, made almost impossible by the present state of the law. The promiscuous homosexual, who seeks his lover in the street, paradoxically runs less risk than the man who lives with another in affection and trust. In such a case, there will always be 'corroborative evidence' of some sort; letters, photographs, the sharing of a home, can always be relied upon to convince a jury when one of the men concerned has been persuaded, by spite, jealousy or fear, to turn Queen's Evidence against the other. I know that this is true, because it is what happened to me. If my interest in McNally had been merely physical, I should never have gone to prison. It was the letters which I had written to him, expressing a deep emotional attachment, which turned the scales against me.

*

I came out into the world again expecting a good deal of hostility. People said to me: 'Now you will really know who your friends are.' Whenever I walked into a room, I waited for the whisper, the snigger or the insult . . . but they never came.

The twenty or thirty people who had been my most intimate friends had never wavered in their loyalty, although until the trial most of them had never guessed the secret which I had so carefully kept from them. They gave me great strength and comfort during the first difficult days, but I realized that I could not live the rest of my life in the shelter of their sympathy and friendship. These men and women, much as I loved them, were not the whole world; and it was the world that I had to face.

When I went to the country to stay with my mother and father, I thought that meeting their friends was going to be the worst ordeal of all. There is probably no group of people more conservative, or less likely to understand a predicament like mine, than the middle-aged inhabitants of a small country town. I knew that they had all been extremely kind to my parents during the time when I was in prison, but this was no indication of their attitude towards me; in fact, I thought it likely that the more they sympathized with my mother and father, the more likely they would be to blame me for their distress. I was surprised and moved to discover that I was quite wrong. Although most of them avoided any discussion of the case, they welcomed me back as though nothing had happened. Of all the people whom I have met since my release, I perhaps appreciate the attitude of these the most, because it meant that they had searched their hearts and discovered there a wealth of humanity and tolerance with which I would never have credited them, and with which they might never have credited themselves.

The third circle into which I now moved was that of the men among whom I had previously worked. It is not easy to go back to Fleet Street when your name and photograph have been displayed on the front page of every newspaper, and I hesitated for some weeks before I did so. Again, I need not have been afraid. The men and women who work in Fleet Street may be cynical in some respects, but they are generous and delightfully frank. There was not a moment of embarrassment, even when I met the reporters who had 'covered' the trial; there was no moral judgement and, I am glad to say, no pity.

I went back to Islington, feeling vaguely apprehensive about the neighbours. I had never spoken to any of them before, and I wondered how they felt about a man with an Oxford accent who came to live among them, re-decorated his house in a manner which probably struck them as obnoxious, and then proceeded to go to gaol. If they had resented my presence there, I thought, they had every opportunity of showing it now. I began to sweep and dust the rooms and clean the windows, feeling rather depressed. After a few minutes the woman next door leaned out of a window and said that it was wonderful to see me back again, and was there anything she could do to help? I thanked her for her kindness and, feeling much better, went to the front door to shake the mat. Another neighbour stopped in the street, smiled, and said: 'Welcome home.' For the rest of the afternoon my work was punctuated by these greetings, and offers of assistance – did I want a hand with the cleaning? Was there any shopping they could do for me? They were just going to the launderette; could they take anything for me? And, like the reporters, they were perfectly open about it all. They did not pretend to think that I had been away in hospital or in Jamaica. They said: 'We read all about it in the papers, and we thought it was a rotten shame.' Nothing in my life has been more heart-warming than this welcome back to the place where I had made my home.

*

That is public opinion, so far as I am able to judge it for myself. I am a homosexual and a convict, but I have been allowed to return; and in that fact there lies a measure of hope for all homosexuals, and for all ex-prisoners. I have moved out of darkness, and into light. I should be untrue to myself if I did not help others to make the same journey.

Two months after my release from Wormwood Scrubs I was sitting, not without an awareness of irony, in the Distinguished Strangers' Gallery at the House of Lords. Below me, on the Woolsack, sat Sir David Maxwell Fyfe, now disguised in knee-breeches, a full-bottomed wig, the title of Viscount Kilmuir and the office of Lord Chancellor. It was hard to believe that this inconspicuous-looking man was one of those who had sent me to prison; I found that I was able to look down at him with no hatred. It was fear that had bred hatred in me, and I had cast them out together.

Lord Pakenham was speaking of his inquiry into the causes of crime. He said: 'I have, I believe, made a number of friends during this inquiry, on both sides of the fence. I include among friends found in that way one or two who have recently been imprisoned and who bear well-known and honoured names, and who have borne themselves, as I have the best reasons for knowing, very bravely in their adversity.'

He said that he would not go into the 'very complex and sometimes very tragic questions associated with homosexuality', which were being investigated by the Government Committee, but that he would like to draw attention to the failure of the prison system to carry out its declared aim, as described by the Chairman of the Prison Commissioners, Sir Lionel Fox: *'The purposes of the training and treatment of convicted prisoners shall be to establish in them the will to lead a good and useful life on discharge, and to fit them to do so.'*

The figure showed, he said, that only about one prisoner in six was receiving any training at all. He called on the Government to match words with deeds, and to reconstruct the

Prison Service in such a way that it might carry out the reforms to which lip-service had been paid for so long.

Peer after peer rose to support him. From the Government benches Viscount Templewood declared: 'We know what ought to be done, but we do not do it. In certain respects, far from making any progress, we have actually fallen back, I would almost say 50 or 60 years.' The practice of locking prisoners up, three to a cell, 'would have horrified the great penal reformers of the past who made our system one of the best in the world'. Nothing was being done to repair the older prisons, and the idea of work in prison was still tainted with the idea of the treadmill – 'we ought to revolutionize our ideas in this respect. Such work should be useful; it should be paid for at the regular rate of wages, and the wages paid should be allocated to the man's keep, to compensation for the victims, and to the accumulation of a sum for the prisoner when he leaves prison. ... I am convinced that the best hope for many of these prisoners, some of whom may at first sight appear to be absolutely hopeless, is to make them work and take an interest in their work.'

I thought of the men whom I had left behind. Of the boredom, the squalor, the sheer nagging hopelessness of it all. The monotony, and the tenpence-a-week.

The Earl of Huntingdon suggested that a man who worked well should earn thereby some remission of his sentence; it was precisely the suggestion that Dan had made, months before, on the exercise yard. It was strange to hear it repeated in this vast Gothic hall, with the chandeliers and the brass rails and the carved gargoyles. The sanitary conditions in some of our prisons, said the Earl, would disgrace a Hottentot village. The system of sewing mailbags in cells at night, with only a 40-watt bulb for illumination, prevented prisoners from reading and ruined their eyesight. Toothache ... epileptics ... censorship of letters ... chamber-pots. The earl was remarkably well-informed. 'If we are to educate prisoners to better standards,' he declared 'it will not be done by sending them into slum conditions.'

Lord Moynihan pointed out that, although this was a matter in which the Church might have interested itself, not a single

Bishop had stayed to listen to the debate. He had heard of Borstal boys who had been asked: 'Are you a Christian?' and had replied: 'No, Church of England.' Many of these boys came from bad homes, 'either with fathers who are criminals themselves, or, much more often, with families who "couldn't care less". They have the wrong friends. They cannot go home to get help, because there is no help there. They get a little worse, and start on a life of crime. When they come out of prison, they go back to exactly the same surroundings. . . . '

I thought of Jimmy, and of Dan; of the penny-in-the-slot machine which had been the first milestone on Dan's journey to the Scrubs – perhaps, eventually, to Dartmoor.

Lord Chorley said: 'There are still in existence gaols which were condemned long before the First World War, and which are not fit to house swine, let alone human beings. . . . '

I looked around at the noble Lords beneath me. Very few of them had bothered to stay. It was half-past six. Of those who remained, several were asleep, their hearing-aids drooping from elderly, blue-veined hands. The visitors' gallery was empty, except for myself. Lord Mancroft, Joint Under Secretary of State for the Home Office, took his feet off the table, glanced at the clock, and rose to make the Government's reply.

He was a smoothly handsome, youngish man in a beautiful suit, who would not have looked out of place in a motor show-room. His purpose this evening, however, was not to sell their Lordships a Jaguar or a Rolls-Royce; it was to sell them an account of the prison administration so grossly ill-informed that I could scarcely prevent myself from unscrewing the nearest brass gargoyle and throwing it at his brilliantined head.

'I will gladly deal with the important points which have been raised,' purred Lord Mancroft; and then proceeded to ignore every unpleasant detail of prison life which had been exposed, ascribing these to 'the sensational crime stories by ex-prisoners which appear in our Sunday newspapers.'

The Earl of Huntingdon had asked why prisoners were made to sew mailbags in their cells at night, when they might have been reading or studying for correspondence courses. Lord Mancroft elegantly sidestepped this by remarking:

'Many prisoners are incapable of anything except simple repetitive work – and that is the answer to the point which the noble Earl made about mailbags; that many prisoners could not handle the more complicated machinery which might be desirable for economic efficiency.' It was, of course, no answer at all. It was not even true. At Wormwood Scrubs there were machines capable of sewing mailbags in a fraction of the time which they took to do by hand, and there was no shortage of prisoners who had been trained to work them. The 'cell-task' was obviously a deliberate time-waster; tread-mill work, as Lord Templewood had said.

'Sanitation,' said the Government spokesman, 'has been mentioned by many noble Lords. Of course, nobody in his right mind would not admit that there is great room for improvement. We have exerted a great deal of effort to try to improve the Victorian sanitary conditions prevailing in prisons, and shall continue to do so. But, barring the pulling down of all prisons, we have done about as much as we possibly can.'

I could spend a pleasant day, I reflected, taking Lord Mancroft on a conducted tour of the latrines at Wormwood Scrubs. We could start by having our breakfast in 'D' Hall, ten feet away from a lavatory whose contents had overflowed on to the floor. Then we could go to the Tailors' Shop, to see what happened when two W.C.s were shared by eighty men. Later, preferably during a blizzard, we could sample those in the exercise yard, listening to the musical hollow clanking which was the only response when one pulled the chain. Finally, we could examine the slopping-out sinks on the landing, forever innocent of disinfectant; and so to bed, with a nice crusty chamber-pot for company.

'Food. . . . ' said Lord Mancroft, with an appetizing smile. 'I want to draw attention to food because, whenever food is bad, or someone complains, it becomes headlines in the newspapers at once. Food is now served in cafeteria trays, and is of a standard which might surprise noble Lords.' Yes, I thought, it probably might, particularly if they knew that the cafeteria trays had been washed in soapless water by prisoners who had not had an opportunity of cleaning their hands after going to the lavatory.

His picture of the facilities for training in prison was rosy and bright. Everyone who could possibly go to a 'training prison' – i.e. about a third of all imprisoned men – went there. The remainder stayed in 'local prisons' like Wormwood Scrubs, either because they were waiting to move on to another prison, or because they were 'quite unsuitable to be sent anywhere else'. I could hardly believe my ears when I heard this, but he went on: 'I do not wish to sing too highly the praises of the local prisons. They tend to become a sort of sump of the prison world, into which all kinds of people who cannot be fitted in anywhere else find their way. But, with this very unpromising material, we are doing the best we can with limited resources, with highly unsuitable buildings, with overcrowding, with under-staffing, and with the necessity to concentrate on discipline and safe custody.'

I had always wondered why the Commissioners had decided that I was to spend the whole of my sentence at Wormwood Scrubs, and now I knew. I was unsuitable, unpromising and unfit for anything but Major Grew's slummy and putrescent sump. So were all the friends I had made in prison. I wondered who made these decisions, and how. I knew that nobody had ever interviewed John, Dan, Charlie, Jimmy, or myself, with a view to discovering whether we were capable of improvement, or of being trained to lead a better life. Vic had been lucky enough to attract the attention of the Governor of a 'prison without bars', who visited the Scrubs occasionally in the manner of a prospective buyer visiting the Battersea Dogs' Home. We were apparently the mongrels whom nobody wanted. It was all right for me, but what about the others?

I suddenly felt ill and tired. I walked down the stairs and along the stone corridors, past the obsequious policeman at the door, and out into the roaring merry-go-round of Parliament Square. The scarlet of the buses hurt my eyes. Men and girls walked together, laughing. The pigeons strutted on the pavement. It was spring again, and the sparrows would be nesting.

*

It has been said that the purposes of punishment are fourfold. The main objects are to deter the wrongdoer and others, and to reform him; the subsidiary objects are to compensate the injured party and to satisfy the indignation of the community. I doubt whether any of these ends are best achieved by prosecution.

I do not believe that a homosexual can be transformed into a heterosexual overnight by the shock of prosecution and imprisonment. The most that can be expected is that he will, while still experiencing an attraction towards his own sex, refrain from giving way to it again. On the other hand, I have never met a homosexual who has resolved to mend his ways as a result of being imprisoned. The laws under which these men are prosecuted appear to them so flagrantly unjust that there is no question of their feeling any remorse or shame for what they have done. This attitude, which may or may not be justified, is strengthened by the fact that no moral stigma attaches to adult homosexuality in the prison community. In this respect it differs from pederasty, or the seduction of boys; and under the combined pressure of disapproval from their fellow-prisoners and perhaps the realization that their actions are morally indefensible, pederasts do sometimes decide that they will never succumb to temptation again. Whether they carry out these resolutions, I do not know.

It must also be remembered that once a man has been taught to look upon himself as a criminal there is a tendency for him to abandon his standards of morality, not only in the respect in which he has been prosecuted, but in others as well. In the unmoral atmosphere of prison, it is easy to look upon all authority as an anonymous and baleful 'They', to be cheated and disobeyed. This, as I have said, was the outlook of men like Dan who had spent all their lives in and out of Borstals and prisons. It was very contagious. Since we were all indiscriminately branded as criminals, we acquired an extraordinary tolerance towards each others' crimes. I was aware of the dangers of this tendency, and fought against it, but I was not always successful.

In most respects I had always been a singularly law-abiding person, paying my taxes, doing my duty in the War, obeying the regulations, respecting the Government, the Crown and the Police. It would not be honest to pretend that I still feel quite the same. It is easy to believe in Justice when you have not been caught up in its workings. It is easy to have faith in politicians, when you have not listened to them lying about issues in which you are vitally concerned. It is easy to believe in the benevolence and incorruptibility of the police, when you have never been a 'wanted' man.

I do not believe that the fact of my imprisonment, or that of Edward Montagu or Michael Pitt-Rivers, will deter a single person from committing acts such as those with which we were charged. Regrettably enough, I believe that the opposite may be true. I have already written about the influence of the Wilde case, and it has often been pointed out that a crime of a sensational nature which receives wide publicity is often followed by a wave of imitations, committed by people of weak intellect whose imaginations have been inflamed by the newspaper reports. After we were arrested and remanded on bail, Edward Montagu and I received many hundreds of letters from such people, including young boys. One boy of 15 used to try to telephone me almost every day during the weeks when I was waiting for the trial to begin. I find this horrifying and am sincerely grieved to think that I may, however unwillingly and indirectly, have been responsible for such a thing.

The homosexual world is, of necessity, compact and isolated. It is also extraordinarily out of touch with reality. I have already mentioned that a number of homosexuals, respected and discreet, were courageous enough to offer evidence to the Home Office Committee when it was set up. These, however, were exceptional. The great majority of the homosexual community shrugged its shoulders, expressed the opinion that the law would never be changed, and carried on with its dangerous and tragic way of life. Our case caused a momentary flutter, and a number of the better-known homosexuals left the country for a time, until they decided that it was safe to return. I am obliged to admit that most homosexuals are furtive and irresponsible, and that if a more tolerant and just attitude towards their condition is ever adopted by this country it will not be through their efforts. On the other hand, they are perhaps not entirely to blame. Their secretiveness and cynicism are imposed upon them by the law as it now stands.

I do not know how far my prosecution acted as a deterrent. Its purpose as an instrument of reform concerns me alone.

Long before I was prosecuted, I had considered the possibility of submitting myself to a 'cure', if any such existed. I had discussed the question with a number of doctors, without ever discovering one who professed to be able to effect any alteration in my sexual bias. Psychiatrists, psychotherapists, psychologists, and psychoanalysts, derive a large part of their incomes from men who fear that their homosexual instincts, if left unchecked, will involve them in prosecution and disgrace. It is not very surprising therefore, that there should be some resistance towards relaxation of the law among the official organizations of the medical profession. But individual doctors, if they are honest, will nearly always admit that there is nothing they can do. There is no magic cure. Extravagant claims were at one time made for treatment by means of sex-hormone injections. It has since been established that, although the injection of female hormones into a man produced a cessation of all desire, whether homosexual or heterosexual, the effect was only temporary and was sometimes accompanied by distressing physical changes. The man thus treated became a kind of hermaphrodite or eunuch, and suffered from the psychological upset natural to such a condition. A homosexual treated with male hormones, however, did not become more of a 'man'; his desires were merely intensified.

Psychotherapists claim that they are able to help in cases where the homosexual bias is weak, or when it is accompanied by self-condemnation or social maladjustment. The course of treatment is bound to take a very long time and cost a great deal of money, and its effects are always uncertain, depending on the willingness of the patient to be cured and the degree of trust which he feels towards his psychiatrist. Ironically enough, this kind of treatment is only likely to be successful with those who have failed to come to terms with their abnormality. With the man who has learned to accept his condition, it is almost certain to be useless.

In spite of this, it might have been possible for me to embark on such a course, if I had not been sent to prison. At Wormwood Scrubs, which is so often pointed out as a centre for the psychological treatment of offenders, the facilities for such treatment were not so much inadequate, as virtually absent. I met many men who had been told by judges that they were being sent for three, or five, or seven years to a place where they would be properly looked after and encouraged to mend their ways; but nothing whatever was being done for them. Out of 1,000 prisoners at the Scrubs, only 11 were receiving psychiatric treatment at the time I was there, and only a small proportion of these were homosexuals. Dr Landers, the Principal Medical Officer, was an intelligent and honest man who admitted the limitations of the system; but I could not help feeling that he would be doing more good if he had devoted his efforts to improving the revolting sanitary conditions of the place, instead of concentrating on the highly problematical redemption of such a small group.

Once I was in prison, as I have described, I was not only not encouraged to take psychological treatment, but actively discouraged. Men in prison, whatever their crime may have been, do not merely remain as bad as they were when they came in; by a visible process of moral erosion which goes on week after week and year after year, they become worse. This is particularly true of sex offenders, and I do not pretend to have been any exception.

The essential reason for my imprisonment had been my tendency to enter into emotional relationships with men who were not, as Mr Roberts would say, my social equals. In prison, I was surrounded by such men. Partly because of the natural tolerance of their class, and partly because of the relaxed moral atmosphere of prison, they expressed no disapproval of my tendencies and appeared to expect that I should choose one of them as a companion; and that is exactly what happened.

There was never any doubt in the minds of the other prisoners – or, for that matter, of the warders – as to the meaning of my friendship for Dan Starling. There was nothing physical in it, because there could not be; but it was a friendship a great deal less selfish and more true than a mere physical attachment would have been.

Strangely enough, it helped me to find some measure of

happiness in prison; and, even more strangely, freedom. I knew that I should never be afraid any more, or angry, or ashamed, whatever might happen to me afterwards.

*

There is not much to be gained from considering the prosecution from the point of view of compensation for the injured, because nobody ever pretended that the smallest harm had been suffered by Reynolds and McNally. On the whole, they did rather well out of it. The police took every possible precaution to see that their photographs did not appear in the press, and as a reward for their behaviour in court they were promised by the Director of Public Prosecutions and the Air Council that no action would ever be taken against them in respect of the homosexual acts with 24 other men which they had admitted. As a result of various sarcastic questions in the House of Commons they were, however, dismissed from the RAF. I do not know what career they took up after this, or where they are.

In all sincerity, I cannot really believe that the case was very successful in 'satisfying the indignation of the community'. It was McNally and Reynolds who were hissed and booed outside the court, not us. The Press comment, as I have shown, was almost uniformly hostile to the manner in which the convictions had been obtained. The Government was finally goaded into setting up a Committee to investigate the antique and savage laws under which we had been charged. When we came out of prison we found, not hostility and ostracism, but sympathy and acceptance from people in every walk of life. As an 'example', the witch-hunt left everything to be desired.

Perhaps the strangest feature of the case – and, indeed, of the law as it stands to-day – was the way in which it placed everyone connected with it in a position which was, to some extent, a false one. The Home Secretary, Sir David Maxwell Fyfe, was obliged to pretend that the 'crime' involved was of such a serious nature that any methods were justifiable, provided that the 'criminals' were brought to book. The Director of Public Prosecutions, Sir Theobald Mathew, in order to obtain convictions against Edward, Michael and me, had to act as though the offences admitted by McNally and Reynolds were, in comparison, trivial. Mr Roberts, QC, was forced to express a horror of homosexuality which contrasted strangely with his conduct of the Croft-Cooke case. Lord Winterton, who had previously called for revision of the laws, was impelled – for reasons known only to himself – to adopt an attitude of hysterical condemnation. The prison officials had to keep up the fiction that I and my friends were criminals; the psychiatrists had to pretend that I was being rightly punished for something which they regarded as an illness.

The effect on me was exactly the opposite. I was able, at last, to move out of a false position and take up a true one. There was no further need for pretence; I could discard the mask which had been such a burden to me all my life.

When I first went to prison, an official asked me: 'Why do you think you were put on this earth? What do you think is the purpose of it all?'

I still do not know what my answer should have been. At that time, I was incapable of giving any. It seemed to me, during those first few days of solitude and degradation, that my life had been a hopelessly unilluminating one, from which no conclusions could be drawn. I was unable to find any moral in what had happened to me. I had tried to lead a good life, doing no harm to anybody, hating no-one and helping those who needed my help. But this had not been enough. When the time came I was not judged by what I had done; I was judged by what I was.

If my life had ended at that moment, it would have been a failure. It was necessary for me to redeem it if I could; to make it mean something, if only to me. A man born with some defect of the body does not try to deny or to conceal his handicap; he acknowledges it, and does the best he can.

That, I decided, was what I must do for myself.

*Some other books which may
interest readers are described on
the following pages*

How to be Happy though Human

W. BÉRAN WOLFE

A387

Life has become complicated. Work is hard and play is not easy. Thought is often painful, and even love has for many become a torment rather than a joy. The author, a well-known psychologist, explains in this stimulating book how the delicate human machine may be kept smoothly running. Each must shape his own personality and adapt his own psychological equipment to his own needs. In the course of the discussion the author touches helpfully on nearly every problem of everyday life, and explains some common failures and mistakes in an encouraging way. He covers problems met with at work, in the family, and in dealing with one's fellows. Every stage of human development from childhood to old age is covered, as are all activities from work to love. Many of the neuroses and complexes we meet with are described, as are the best methods of dealing with them in oneself or in others.

The Queen's Courts

PETER ARCHER

A 365

The British genius for government, which has combined democracy and personal freedom with orderly adminis-tration, owes much to English ideas of law. These in turn are the products of the legal profession. And that system has been determined less by abstract speculation than by the practical working of the law courts.

An account of the institutions which produced the criminal trial for the protection of the citizen against unlawful interference alike by wrongdoers and the police, and the civil action for the effecting of justice between citizens, is not a static picture. English law em-bodies generations of experience, but it is constantly adapting itself to new situations, and the twentieth century has witnessed the birth of numerous tribunals which have taken their place alongside the ancient courts.

Of all these, their work, and their place in English life, this book sets out to tell. It concludes with a comparison between the legal institutions of this country and those which function in different settings for different ways of life.